TIME TO DECLARE

TIME TO DECLARE
an autobiography

Basil D'Oliveira

With Patrick Murphy

J. M. Dent & Sons Ltd
London Toronto Melbourne

First published 1980
© Basil D'Oliveira and Patrick Murph, 1980

Printed by
Biddles Ltd, Guildford, Surrey, for
J. M. Dent & Sons Ltd
Aldine House, Welbeck Street, London

British Library Cataloguing in Publication Dat

D'Oliveira, Basil
  Autobiography.
  1. D'Oliveira, Basil
  2. Cricket players – Biography
  796.358'092'4   GV915.D6

  ISBN 0–460–04511–3

Contents

List of Illustrations

Between pages 100 and 101

Foreword by John Arlott

Basil D'Oliveira's autobiography is the ultimate success story. It provides comfort and hope for non-white-skinned people of many races in South Africa; offering them evidence that no government can completely cut off their right to prove themselves. This is not simply a matter of sport. There have been few comparable achievements in any field. Of course the nineteenth-century 'improving' book pattern of 'Log Cabin to White House' has been repeated. That, though, was a theme of worthy progress in a society which granted freedom of opportunity.

This is an account of an ascent in face of odds. What opportunity was there for a boy cricketer, denied by the laws of his native country organized coaching; parental financial capacity to afford proper gear; the use of a grass wicket or a safe outfield; the opportunity to take part in a first-class match or to play against opponents experienced at such a level? In fairness it must be said that Basil D'Oliveira's brief glimpse of white men's cricket and cricketing conditions in South Africa was due entirely to the fairmindedness of the white cricketers of that country; it was not snuffed out by them.

When all that is said, consider the chances even now, in 1980, as this is being written, of one of the star-conscious, highly critical and understandably demanding, Lancashire league clubs engaging a Cape Coloured South African with no experience of top level competitive play and no figures of achievement against recognized opposition, as their professional. Yet the success of Basil D'Oliveira in England has made that prospect vastly more attractive than it was in 1960, when his engagement by Middleton was a huge improbability – if not a miracle – springing from a series of accidents and coincidences. It was not simply that Middleton decided not to re-engage Roy Gilchrist as their professional and negotiated with Wesley Hall to take his place. Hall, in his usual conscientious fashion, consulted the West Indian authorities for a considerable period before he decided that he could not accept the offer. By that time it was desperately close to the beginning of the season; quite exceptionally late to open negotiations with another professional. By a freakish coincidence this was John Kay's own club. Only two days before he had received yet another of my importuning letters on behalf of the obscure South African. He suggested that Middleton should engage the unknown and to their eternal credit – and momentously in the course of cricket history – they took that apparently wild risk.

Such was this unusual man's quality, as natural cricketer and human being, that such a glimpse of opportunity was enough. Still, though, all those concerned – Basil himself, John Kay and myself – stand back, yet, in amazement at the thought that it ever happened.

He became a naturalized British subject, and his natural ability, quickly developed technical capacity, admirable temperament, and fundamental courage, established him among English Test cricketers. For Worcestershire he proved an outstanding performer in the years of their highest achievement. Throughout the world of cricket his honesty and good nature made him many friends. At times of stress – as admitted by the MCC establishment under fire for its abandonment of opposition to apartheid – he behaved with the utmost dignity. Now, characteristically, modestly doubtful of his ability to teach others, he embarks on the career of his original choice, but on a more exalted level than he can ever have anticipated, as chief coach to the Worcestershire County Cricket Club which proved his final springboard to fame.

Pat Murphy has served Basil well; for he has written the man as the man is. This book is a true, unvarnished story. It is extremely valuable for adjusting the balance by giving Basil D'Oliveira's true opinion on his 'fact finding' tour of South Africa with the party under Mr Richard Jeeps. Unfortunately his car broke down on his way to the press conference after that visit and he was quoted, at second hand, as passing opinions he neither held nor stated, and which saddened many of his best friends both in this country, and perhaps even more deeply, among his own people in South Africa. Here, on page 152, he uses the opportunity to state what he was prevented – by the accident of a car breakdown – from saying. It must be hoped that his own genuine statement will be as widely repeated as that made 'for him'.

Essentially this is a happy story; the success of an ordinary, honest man of high cricketing gifts against the forces of racism, his passage to freedom, taking his wife and children with him; and his example to millions of others of his kind and country that the path to liberty, though difficult, can be traversed.

Preface

One autumn in the mid-1970s, I was sitting on a beach in Spain with my wife and two sons, minding my own business. The cricket season seemed a million miles away – until a camera crew for Spanish television descended upon us and asked me for an interview. I protested that nobody played cricket in Spain, only to be told – 'Yes, but we know all about you.'

A lot of people know about me for events that happened *off* the cricket field but I can't really complain, for I hope somehow my own life has helped the cause of racial tolerance. Certainly I have no bitterness in my heart as I look back on a career that's now over, a career that's taken me to the kind of places I could only dream about as I lived the ordinary life of a Cape Coloured in Signal Hill, Cape Town. I'm still an ordinary person, despite the millions of words that have been written about me, and I hope this book will confirm that.

I'm grateful to my good friend Pat Murphy for his assistance in setting the tangled parts of my life into one coherent book. To my countless friends, former colleagues and my family I offer sincere thanks for your guidance, respect, affection and love.

Basil D'Oliveira, May 1980.

Dedication

To the late 'Benny' Bansda. Without his many kindnesses,
I would probably still be working at a printers' in Cape Town.

1 Early Days

For more years now than I care to remember, one question keeps cropping up. 'If you had the choice,' I'm asked, 'where would you like to have been born?' My honest answer is always 'England'. I'm proud of my colour, of what I've achieved for myself and non-whites all over the world and I dearly love my own people in Cape Town – but I can't deny that I would have been a better person and cricketer if I'd been born a coloured Englishman. The educational, social and sporting opportunities in England are fabulous compared to those I and millions of others like me experienced in South Africa – and the same applies today, despite the encouraging trends I see every time I return to my homeland.

Like any other proud parent, I've watched the development of my eldest son, Damian, into a fine all-round sportsman. He's now on the MCC Ground Staff at Lord's and, who knows, another D'Oliveira may become a force in the English first-class game. No one will be more delighted than his father if he makes the grade, but he doesn't need me to tell him that if he was still living in the land where he was born, the lack of facilities and opportunities would have slowed his progress. Now, as I watch him hitting a cricket ball as if he hates it, or trying a 25 yard shot with his usual optimism and strong left foot, I often think back to those days when I was trying to break out of the social and sporting straitjacket imposed by the colour of my skin.

If I have one overwhelming regret in my life, it's that the best years of my cricket career weren't properly utilized. Of course I became a better player when I came to England and started learning about a game that had always seemed so uncomplicated to me, but in terms of eyesight, co-ordination, instinct and fitness, I was at my peak while playing with non-whites in the 1950s. My wife, Naomi, has often said I went to England at the right time, because she feels my determination then to succeed was overwhelming and that I might not have developed as a player if things had been easier. But I

1

still had to make the best of what was left. I'd dearly love to have competed on equal terms with the Procters, the Barlows and the Pollocks . . . at the same age, with the same coaching facilities.

I never really knew why I had to play on matting wickets with the most rudimentary grasp of the game and the equipment to match; I vaguely had the impression that we were different from the whites, that we didn't see much of each other and that on the rare occasions when my club played a white team, it was under conditions of secrecy. But I only lived for cricket and soccer so life outside the warm, friendly Signal Hill area of Cape Town didn't really concern me.

I was born a Cape Coloured, one of South Africa's four major groups (the others are white, African and Indian). In those days the various groups had their own sides, although all except the whites would play each other in representative matches, where the atmosphere and the competition would always be needle-sharp. I played for my father's club, St Augustine's, on a vast open space a few miles from both the sea and Cape Town. Looking back on it, the conditions we played under were a tribute to our fanatical love for cricket: about 25 teams shared the same open space and we had to tend the matting wicket ourselves. On the morning of a match I'd walk about ten miles from my home to help prepare the wicket. We'd roll it, water it so it would cake hard on top, nail the matting down on the caked mud and then place boulders and stones on it to keep it down while we changed for the match. We had to be that careful because animals of all shapes and sizes as well as people would happily walk over our precious wicket unless we covered it!

So many teams played on this space that you would often get thumped in the back by a ball from another game; the batsmen regularly hit sixes because the ball was deemed 'lost' in the thick grass. It was also a six if you cleared the electric cables! And the ball would often do crazy things as it careered from boulder to rock from a batsman's stroke. Even if we understood such weighty matters like how to use the seam and to swing the ball, it wouldn't have mattered because the ball was soon knocked out of shape by those rocks. We would play with a ball until its cover came off – then we'd use the cork.

Only when the string unravelled was it time to buy another ball. And whenever you won a cricket award you always said, 'forget the trophy, please can I have a bat?' and then, years later, it would still be your pride and joy, even though it was taped all over.

We were never coached. We used to practise in the streets of Signal Hill, where some of us would be hauled off to jail by the police if we were caught playing on the road. It was in one of these streets that I learned to play fast bowling. My friends would bounce a tennis ball down at me from the stairs leading on to the street and I'd try to swat the ball as it whistled round my ears. So when I started trying to defend myself on matting wickets where the ball bounced viciously, I was used to it.

Our cricket was completely uninhibited by tactical thoughts or other subtleties. The two fastest bowlers would run in and try to hit the batsmen and they in turn would do their best to hammer them out of sight. Knocks were given and taken, none of us had a clue about field-placings and the spinners didn't know how to grip the ball. But cricket was our religion.

After all these years, I still don't know why it was *me* who managed to break through from that tightly-knit cricket community. The advice and encouragement I got were crucial, but the truth is there were more talented players than me playing in those games in Signal Hill. Perhaps they didn't have my deep, burning desire for success; every minute of the day I wanted to play cricket or soccer. I left school at 15 with no academic qualifications and worked as a printer in a stationery firm but my thoughts never really homed in on the techniques of printing. I was too wrapped up in sport.

My determination to succeed at cricket came from my father. He was a good club player and would never suffer excuses from me about my own performance – whenever I failed, I'd think, 'God, what am I going to tell him?' and it was even worse if he was at the game; on the way home, his total silence would make it clear how disgusted he was with me. He could always tell if I wasn't training hard enough and, years later, when I became an established England player, he'd write, 'I've told you to stop hitting the ball in the air, fancy getting out to a bowler like that.' And if I dropped a catch – well that was unforgivable! He never praised me and I remained in awe of him till his death in 1979 – but I loved and respected him and owe him so much.

Although we Coloureds had little to do with white people, I eventually wanted to find out more about their style of play and facilities. Whenever possible, I'd go to Newlands, Cape Town's famous stadium, to watch the great white players in Test matches. I'd sit in the segregated part of the ground, blissfully unconcerned that I couldn't sit beside a white man but terribly envious at the skills on display. I could only afford to go for one day – I'd clean my father's pigeon loft to earn my shilling for admission and walk the seven miles to the ground. Was I envious! I'd look at the lush outfield and the beautiful wicket and wonder what it would be like to divorce myself from playing in a park where about twenty different games were going on simultaneously – just for one day, please God, to play here. But that was one dream I was never allowed to realize.

I'd be sitting down by deep fine leg and gods like Peter May, Denis Compton, Colin Cowdrey, Neil Adcock and Hugh Tayfield would come and pick up the ball. How clean, fresh, athletic and . . . white they all looked! I'd read everything about them and there they stood, just a few yards away. I wasn't bitter or resentful that certain things were denied me because of my colour; I was simply sad that I would never get a chance to play at Newlands. But I always supported the visiting country – after all, they weren't denying me the chance to play in such a magnificent stadium.

But I never had a hatred for the white man. I knew about the laws of the land, about the 'separate development' policy that became Government policy in 1948, and we would have been foolish at that time if we had tried to buck the system. We understood why we had to stay in the same railway compartment for two days whenever we travelled to play soccer in Johannesburg or Port Elizabeth, why we never saw a white man on the journey, why we had our own toilets and restaurants. The Government said so. I had no desire to exchange my cricket bat and soccer boots for a gun.

I must have had some natural talent because I began to put together some impressive cricketing achievements. I can't

1 Practice in Cape Town, in the late 1950s.

2 The Mayor of Cape Town presents me with a local newspaper award for being one of the Sportsmen of the Year.

3 and 4 Wedding day, 1960 – and Naomi and myself 20 years later.

6 With Alf Gover's side in Pakistan, 1963. In case you can't spot me, I'm 4th on the left.

5 Middleton, 1960 and my first landlord and landlady – Mary and Clarence Lord – at no. 53 Rochdale Road, Middleton.

8 Johannesburg, 1967 – and the cricket-mad Indians want to know everything about playing for England.

7 Even the nuns wanted to know about cricket when I came back to South Africa to coach in 1967.

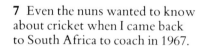

9 and **10** Back for a guest appearance with my old club, St Augustine's in Cape Town. The quality of the matting wickets and the bumpy outfield hadn't changed at all!

have been all that bad because I scored 80 centuries in nine years of non-European cricket in South Africa. Once I scored 225 in 70 minutes and on another occasion, I hit 46 off an 8-ball over. Another time I took 9 for 2 with my off-breaks – even then I was conning batsmen out! As a batsman, I just tried to smash the ball out of sight and I loved playing for the Coloureds against the Malays, the Indians and the Bantus in national tournaments.

It started to dawn on me that I wasn't a bad cricketer when I played for non-white South Africa against the Kenya Asians in 1956. We beat them in all three 'Tests' and they were so impressed that they asked us to go out there and play them in 1958. We played 16 matches on that tour under my captaincy and we lost only once. We were a really good side, the first non-Europeans to tour outside South Africa, and I think we shook a few people in East Africa. The opposition was nearly of first-class standard and I averaged 46 with the bat and took 25 wickets cheaply.

By this time, enthusiasm for cricket was massive in the non-white communities of South Africa and I realized that this was the way I could better myself. As there was no point in expecting the apartheid laws to be repealed, I had to prove my point that we were as good as anybody in the only place I felt at ease – the cricket field. We even tried to get Frank Worrell to bring his West Indian Test side over to play us in South Africa; in those days, such an informal trip would not have been frowned on, as long as the West Indians kept away from the whites. Excitedly we talked long into the night about asking Frank to 'throw' one of the games, so that the publicity about our victory would reach a wider audience – but our hopes were dashed when the tour was called off for no apparent reason.

By January, 1960, I was finished with cricket. The cancellation of the West Indies tour seemed to end my chances of making a name for myself. I'd received great local publicity over the years for my runs and wickets but I realized I had to try my luck against tougher opposition if I was ever going to develop as a player. There seemed little hope of that. The thought of playing in England had nagged away at me for several years, and in 1958, I had plucked up courage to write to John Arlott, the famous BBC cricket broadcaster. English cricket and John Arlott had always been synonymous to me. I read everything I could find about the English Test and county players and hung on every word of Mr Arlott whenever I heard his radio commentaries in Cape Town. His voice and the words he spoke convinced me that he was a nice, compassionate man so I started writing to him, asking him if there was any chance at all of playing cricket in England for a living. Characteristically, he wrote regular, sympathetic and encouraging letters to me, but we kept coming up against the same brick wall. Years later, he told me how difficult it was to convince English clubs that a man who'd picked up wickets and scored many runs in non-white South African cricket could be a good investment on soft, English wickets. I had no experience of first-class cricket, I wasn't exactly in the first flush of youth and there was no indication that I could be a crowd-puller in England. I can't say I was surprised but it did nothing to lift the depression that surrounded me after the West Indian trip was cancelled. So in January, 1960, I took the step that in my own mind sealed my disenchantment with cricket – I got married. Naomi and I had grown up together and we always knew we would marry one day – but during our courtship I seemed to be out training and playing sport all the time. So when we decided to marry, I knew I was loosening cricket's hold over me.

A month later, however, a letter came from England that changed my life. It was from John Arlott. After two years of trying, he had achieved the seemingly impossible – a contract for the unknown D'Oliveira in the Central Lancashire League with Middleton. It was just for one season and the money was only £450 but, for a few triumphant hours, that didn't matter. I blessed the names of John Arlott, of the editor of *World Sports*, the British magazine that ran a feature on my career at the same time that the Middleton officials were debating whether to offer me a contract, and I blessed all my friends who'd told me not to despair.

But within a few hours reality dawned. Only £450? And I had to pay my own air fare of £200 out of that? And my digs out of the remaining £250? Not a hope, I thought – and on top of all that, I'd just learned that my wife was pregnant. That's when I found out who were my true friends. Naomi said, 'Bas, you'll never forgive yourself if you give up now', and then three men – an Indian, a Cape Coloured and a Muslim – took up my cause and by their own efforts put me on that plane to England.

Damoo Bansda, known to everyone as 'Benny', was the Indian. He was a sports writer, and a part-time barman, and a man who never stopped encouraging me to spread my cricketing wings. It was Benny who sent a list of my performances to *World Sports* magazine, it was he who would write kindly about me, never doubting that I would make the grade somehow. So when I realized I couldn't afford to go to England, I sought out Benny. He was working in a whites-only bar and I slipped in through the back door to avoid police attention. 'Don't worry, Bas, we'll get you there,' he told me, 'and don't worry about Naomi's pregnancy, my family will take care of her.' He was as good as his word. He and my brother-in-law, Frank Brache and a Muslem friend, Ishmail Adams, formed a committee to raise funds for my trip. They encountered some opposition from blacks and Coloureds who felt I should know my place, stay with my own people and keep out of the white man's world. I felt I could do something for my own people on a larger stage than Signal Hill, Cape Town, and luckily most of the locals agreed with me.

Within a month, my friends raised £450 for me. One match alone fetched £150, and I often use this game as a reason for my tolerant attitude to all races, despite things that have happened to me because of my colour. Gerald Innes, a former first-class cricketer, told me he was putting a game on for me at a local club and he was bringing along players like Peter Van der Merwe, who was later to captain South Africa in England. 'Never mind the laws, Bas', he told me, 'we'll get you to England.' Gerald was as good as his word and it was a wonderful sight to see him and his white team-mates join Benny and my Coloured friends in walking round the ground with buckets filled with coins.

How can I thank those people of all creeds and colours for defying the apartheid laws to get me to England? If Gerald Innes and his white colleagues had been dyed-in-the-wool Afrikaaners, they wouldn't have been so willing to help a bloke from the Cape Coloured community and I doubt if my own intimate group of friends would then have scratched together the necessary cash in time. In the next couple of decades, more and more pressure was to be placed on my shoulders from militant groups of all varieties – and whenever the black militants pressed me for a definitive anti-white statement, I would think of the friendly whites who helped me so much.

So at last I had the money. But the misgivings still refused to dissolve. Was I good enough? Would I be going half-way round the world to be a laughing stock, letting my people down? How could I look them in the face again if I came back from Middleton within a few weeks? I realized I needed some guidance about playing cricket in England, particularly the Lancashire League. Again, help came from a white man – Tom Reddick, a former Nottinghamshire player who'd coached in Lancashire and knew every nook and cranny of the League system. A sweet, gentle man, he devoted that last crucial month of March to me; he talked and talked about the English game and I took in as much of it as I could. Every day he gave me coaching lessons in his backyard – I'd never been coached for even five minutes, nor played on a grass wicket yet here he was, telling me about the bounce of the wickets in Lancashire, the poor light, the fact that, as a professional, I would be a marked man because I was expected to do well.

At the end of the coaching session, he invited me into his house for an orange juice. I couldn't believe the kindness, dedication and respect he showed me. I wasn't used to this from a white man and I'll never forget him – nor the words he uttered to me years later when I saw him again after I'd played for England. 'Do you know, Bas,' he said, 'when you came to me in 1960, I wanted to tell you to stay at home and be a big fish in a small pool. I didn't think you had a chance of making it in England, yet you were so enthusiastic and keen to learn that I didn't have the heart to speak my mind. I still can't believe that you've done so much because each stage you passed through was surely the last one you'd master. But you kept proving me wrong and made me realize that you can always be wrong in this game.'

At the end of March, 1960, I boarded a plane for England,

frightened out of my wits – not least because it was only the second plane trip of my life. My bride of three months promised she would write every day, my friends and relatives kept telling me I was sure to be a great success – yet the cautionary words of Tom Reddick kept swirling around in my confused mind. Within a few months, I would be a father for the first time; what kind of future could I guarantee Naomi and my child? As I dragged myself away from my family, an old aunt said something to me that has stayed in my mind ever since – 'aim high, Basil, there's room for everybody up there.' I hope I didn't disappoint her.

2 The English Experience

April 1st, 1960, will always remain the most astonishing day of my life. Of course, there have been other, more publicized days which would seem to qualify but none can compare to the series of shocks I received to my naive, insular system on that cold, damp April day when my plane landed in London.

On the flight over I didn't sleep a wink. I kept thinking, 'My God what have I let myself in for? I don't know anybody, why didn't I stay with my friends?' It was only my second flight on a plane and I was ill-prepared for such a marathon journey – with just my misgivings and my inferiority complex for company. When we landed, I stumbled down the steps, trying to adjust to the kind of gloom and dampness I'd never experienced and wondering why there were so many photographers clicking away at the passengers. Then I got the shock of my life as this white chap said, 'Will you look this way, Mr D'Oliveira?' I wasn't sure what surprised me more – the fact that a white man was so polite to me or that it was my picture they were after! I stood there, freezing like the Abominable Snowman, thinking to myself, 'Is this all a practical joke?', then the air hostess stuck a note in my hand. It was from John Kay, the Manchester journalist who'd acted on John Arlott's recommendation and got me fixed up with the Middleton club. 'I'm waiting for you inside,' the note said, 'and don't say anything to anybody.' John greeted me warmly in the airport and then I was whisked into a television interview room. By this time, I was in a complete daze. All this was surely happening to somebody else and I was simply on the outside observing it. Huge, bright lights were switched on, I did the interview and I shudder to imagine what I said to the camera; my command of English was, to say the least, elementary and I felt inadequate and lonely. Is this what Benny and my friends collected all that money for? To make me feel humiliated in front of all these sophisticated people?

Things improved, though, when I was taken to meet John Arlott. He was just as his voice had led me to believe – sympathetic and sincere yet with a sense of humour ('You look just like a Pakistani, Basil', he said). John gave me some words of encouragement and then it was time to get to Middleton. I, of course, had no idea how we would manage that but luckily, John Kay was in command. We caught a train and that's when I had my next shock. 'Time for a bite to eat,' said John. I agreed and I settled back expecting to eat in our own compartment. After all that's what I was used to in South Africa. Not a bit of it – I was taken to the restaurant car where a lot of white people were sitting, blissfully unconcerned by the presence of a coloured man from the Cape. I was frightened out of my wits, I felt I was infringing vital laws and customs but John kept saying, 'Don't worry about it Basil, you're in a different country now. No one can harm you for eating with white men.'

But I still felt totally bewildered and out of my depth and the feeling only started to decrease when we arrived at Manchester. The club officials greeted me like a long-lost brother and even though I was still astonished that these cheerful, warm-hearted people were white, I was touched by their sincerity. By this time I was on my knees with exhaustion but I was whisked off to a golf club in Middleton for a dinner in my honour. Imagine that – a big, posh, grand affair for a bloke from half-way round the world who probably couldn't play the game in the English manner! I stood in the dining room, shyly acknowledging the welcomes and hospitality, wondering how far my command of the English language was likely to extend when I saw a box with a glass front on it in the corner. I asked what it was and the answer came – 'A television. Haven't you seen one before?' Of course I hadn't and when it was switched on and I saw my favourite football team (Manchester United) on the screen within a couple of minutes, the world felt a better place. I sat glued to the screen while all around me there was talk and laughter. Looking back, I must have seemed an ungracious newcomer to the warm-hearted surroundings, but my life until then had been sheltered and limited, and after my flight from South Africa, all these eye-opening incidents were just too much for my simple mind.

Eventually – shattered and cold – I was taken to my digs at number 53 Rochdale Road, Middleton. I'll never forget the number of that house, nor the welcome and hospitality that greeted me from Clarence Lord, a Lancastrian to his toes, and his wife, Mary, an Irish lass with a heart as big as Manchester. Mary took one look at me, parked me by the fire and proceeded to tell me not to worry anymore. She tucked me up in bed with a hot water bottle and seemingly hundreds of blankets and told me not to get up until I felt like it. At that moment, I felt like sleeping till Christmas.

The next day, dear old Mary protected me from the press with all the fierce instincts of a mother hen. I got up just after midday and as I looked out at the cold, dank weather my spirits sank to new depths. Had I travelled from sunny Cape Town for this? How could I do myself justice on the cricket field when it was so cold? Unknown to me, there was a man downstairs who would soon answer that question. His name was Roy Gilchrist, a West Indian cricketer who'd had his share of notoriety at the hands of the press and some players. Roy had just finished as Middleton's professional and when he heard I'd arrived, he came round to offer some advice to his successor. 'You don't know me,' he said, 'but I want you to come out with me this afternoon and we'll have a talk.' Well, he did the talking and I just listened; he told me all about the English wickets, about the club's officials, the way that League cricket is organized, how to behave like a professional and that I would be up against it if I didn't deliver the goods on the field. His advice that day was invaluable. Of course I had heard of Roy Gilchrist – he'd played 13 times for the West Indies – and I knew all about his turbulent temperament and his habit of bowling 'beamers' at batsmen he disliked. But there was no need for him to go out of his way on my behalf and I've never forgotten him for that. Roy Gilchrist can come and knock on my door anytime.

But for all his kindness, Roy couldn't hold my hand when I tried to play cricket. I was an absolute disaster in those early weeks at Middleton. After just a few days in the nets, I realized I knew nothing about this game. I'd been used to hitting the ball as far as possible and expecting a fast bowler to try to knock my block off. I'd never seen the ball swing through the air before and the ball kept 'stopping' so I was through with my shot far too early with the ball going straight up in the air.

I was a novice and what's more, everyone knew it. The welcome I received from all the players, the local press and Club officials was tremendous – but I knew what they were all saying in those first few weeks: 'This guy's a waste of money, he can't play in English conditions.' In my heart of hearts, I didn't disagree with them but I wasn't going to show it. All my life I've been a great one for practising in the nets and I started to watch how the good players in the club coped with the ball that seamed off the wicket or swung through the air. They would let the ball come to them, rather than chase it, and instead of slogging at everything, they would wait for the bad ball and then whack it. There was very little front-foot driving because the wickets were so damp that the ball would be swinging and slowing down once it pitched.

I practised and practised – yet I was still a disaster when it came to the actual games. In my first five matches I made a grand total of 25 runs! I was desperately homesick, I wrote to Naomi that I was coming back and although everyone kept encouraging me, I knew they were terribly disappointed with the professional who'd been engaged with money that they'd provided by subscriptions and hard fund-raising work. In those first few desperate weeks, the four walls in my bedroom were my only real companions. I used to come home from the nets in the evening, still brooding about my latest failure at the weekend and talk out loud to myself in my room. What was I doing wrong? Why couldn't I play this game? When can I go home? Why can't I talk things over with these lovely people in Middleton? In those days, I was a very shy person (basically I still am despite the front I put up) and because of my narrow upbringing and my sensitivity about my colour, it took me a long time to break down the barriers of my natural reserve. I was too introverted to ask advice, I wanted to sort it out myself and silence the doubters I'd hear expressing their derogatory opinions about my talents as I walked through the club bar after yet another poor performance. It was getting embarrassing because one of my duties as club professional involved coaching the youngsters in the afternoon and then the senior players at night. What a joke, I could hear them say – the coach who can't even sort out his own game!

Then – just like many other critical times in my life – I

had a stroke of luck. I got some good advice from a man I'd
been too shy to ask. Eric Price had been a fine slow left-arm
bowler for Lancashire and Essex in his day and now, with
Middleton, he was still a master craftsman. He was a former
pro with the club and I couldn't blame him if he thought, 'pro
cricket is a hard school, he's got to learn for himself.' But he
didn't, bless his heart, and on the way to those early matches
he'd talk to me about the techniques needed to play the game
in England. 'Wait and relax,' he'd say, 'the weather will get
better and the wickets harder. Till then, you've got to wait for
the ball to come to you and work it away off the back foot.
And your bowling is far too short. Pitch it up. If you keep
dropping it short, they'll murder you because you're just not
sharp enough.' Basically Eric was saying, 'pull your finger out
and think about your profession', and his advice was invaluable. In the next match, I got 78 against Werneth on a lovely
sunny day and a good wicket. I never looked back after that
knock. I kept applying myself and saying, 'you've got to do it,
you've got to do it,' as I walked to the wicket. I can well
understand how Geoff Boycott got so wrapped up in cricket. I
think I was a bit like him in those early days at Middleton – I
didn't drink, so I couldn't go and drown my sorrows in the
bar and wake up the next day with just a hangover and
nothing else to worry about. I wasn't a good mixer for a variety of reasons, I had no wife at home to discuss things with,
and I would sit in my digs at night and mope if I'd failed in that
day's play – all the while wishing the rest of the week away so
I could get a chance to make amends. I was as dedicated as
Geoff Boycott in those days and that's why I've never criti-
cised him for the things he's given up to reach such a high
level. Indeed, I admire him for such dedication.

Although my frustrations and periods of deep depression
were many in that 1960 season, there were two big plusses: I
scored nearly a thousand runs and took 70-odd wickets but,
more importantly, I finished top of the averages in the Central
Lancashire League, ahead of Gary Sobers. Now averages have
honestly never bothered me apart from that season, when I
was determined to top Sobers. I'd met him a couple of times
that season (he was playing for Ratcliffe) and although he was
like a god to me, I was determined to try to beat him in the

averages. All my life, I've aimed for a particular target because even if I fail to reach it, at least I'll have attained a level of competence trying for it. It's better than just jogging along. So I aimed for Sobers, which was ridiculous considering he was such a great all-rounder and I was a novice. I kept looking for his performances every week in the local paper, hoping that I'd topped him in the previous match – but I found out later from the Ratcliffe lads, that Gary did the same for me! I thought it unbelievable that Gary should concern himself with the efforts of someone like me – but I found it a tremendous compliment. I was beginning to realize how far one could go if the attitude was right. Mind you, it just shows how deceptive statistics can be.

So Middleton were pleased with me at the end of the 1960 season and they offered to pay the air fares of myself and Naomi to return for the 1961 season. I was delighted to accept. At that time I thought, 'Well I can't go on much longer but at least I'm making progress in League cricket. I haven't let my people down.' County cricket was the last thing on my mind as I travelled back to Cape Town to encounter yet another astonishing surprise in a year of amazing events. I had no idea that any news of my exploits had filtered back to South Africa but when I sat giving interviews for three hours to the press before getting off the boat, I realized I hadn't disappointed my people. My wife and family were waiting for me at the quayside and as soon as I got off the boat, I was whisked off to an open-car welcome down the main street of Cape Town and a civic reception with the Lord Mayor. Things had certainly changed and if I had had any wry reflections about my changed status with the white men who were now cheering me so hoarsely, I kept them to myself. After all, many whites had helped fund my trip to Middleton and I'd just come from a land where the white man had treated me with respect. But deep down, I knew my success had been for my own people on Signal Hill, for those who'd played with and against me and those from the same background. They shared in my success and I was proud for them, and I was astonished at how much they knew about my performances for Middleton. One thing bothered me, though, as the back-slapping and the genuine welcomes rained down on me: would my people want me to play cricket again on those matting wickets? I'd thought about that on the trip back and I realized that I couldn't afford to lapse into my old bad habits on the cricket field, now that I'd made some progress towards understanding the game as it was played on grass. I told them how hard it had been in those early weeks at Middleton, how I was so near to being a shameful disaster, that I couldn't afford to change my style again. I shouldn't have worried – they were understanding and encouraging. Nobody pressurized me and I only played a couple of games for my old club on grass.

One other incident marred my enjoyment on that delightful day. My wife was heavily pregnant at that time and, while waiting for me to escape the well-meaning clutches of the press, she wanted to go to the toilet. The toilet was right beside her at the docks but a policeman wouldn't let her go in . . . because she wasn't white. Seven months pregnant, she had to stagger another 500 yards to the non-white toilet. When I heard about that, I was really annoyed and I still haven't forgotten it. Little things like that made me realize what a civilized country England was and I looked forward to bringing up my children in an atmosphere where the colour of one's skin was irrelevant.

By the spring of 1961, Naomi and I were in Middleton, the proud parents of a newly-born son. Naomi and Damian, unwittingly, were a great help to me as I tried to get used to the English way of life and cast aside my reserve, my protective outerskin. Naomi has always been an open, friendly woman with a great love of home life and she soon slipped into the free and easy atmosphere of Middleton. But even she had difficulty in adjusting at the start – we'd walk down the street and she'd say, 'Do you see that?' as a white girl walked hand-in-hand with a black man; she would gasp in astonishment as the kind folk of Middleton would come up to the wife of their cricket club's professional and introduce themselves, offering any help or advice that we might need. And when we went to the pictures, she couldn't believe what she saw; she assumed we would have to sit in a separate part of the cinema and whenever the lights went up in the interval, she would die the death. She would grip my arm so tightly with tension that it would be bruised the next day.

Gradually she realized that these people were as friendly as they seemed. Initially she felt the same as me, that we had no right to be in their society; but soon she had made contact with all the local housewives in the shops and before long she had friends all over the place. We bought a little 'two up, two down' for about £400 and we thought it was a palace – flagstones in the kitchen, the bath up against the wall and an outside toilet. We'd sit cuddling in front of the fire to keep warm and then some of the lads from the club brought us an old carpet, a second-hand three-piece suite, some curtains and crockery. And when I found out at the end of the 1961 season that I could get a council grant to help me pay for modernizing the house – well, I just couldn't believe it. There I was, a resident of Middleton for hardly five minutes, yet people were nagging me to go and ask the council for a £250 grant. And when the council agreed, I said to Naomi, 'This is one hell of a country!'

We made friends with a lovely couple of spinsters who simply took Damian to their hearts. Elsie and Jessie Taylor were both in their seventies; their front door backed on to the foot of our back garden and they used to take Damian for walks and show him off to everyone. They were a lovely couple of ladies who did so much for us, even down to helping Damian perfect his Lancashire accent!

Gradually my confidence grew and I was flattered that so many people were asking my opinion about life in South Africa. I was still very guarded, still feeling my way along and hoping that my deeds on the cricket field would be the talking point, rather than politics. I still knew my place and didn't speak very fluently but I was developing a deep admiration for the English – for their respect for privacy, their honesty, their willingness to do favours without expecting anything in return. There was Frank Lomas, for instance, a great lad, who used to drive me to matches after he'd finished his day's work of selling baby wear. Frank was also a fanatical Manchester United supporter and we would go to Old Trafford whenever possible. I still see him today; he runs a pub in Cambridge and I was delighted to give him a reference when he wrote to the brewery. It was a pleasure to give something back at last to someone from that cosy, warm town of Middleton.

Life wasn't all cricket in those days, either. I had a variety of jobs – in a printer's, an engineering firm and then a packing warehouse. I worked from seven in the morning till eight at night when I wasn't playing cricket and I was contented. My family were happy, I was starting to earn good money for them and I was learning how to play the difficult game of English cricket. I was learning how to delay my shots till the last possible second, to punch the ball off the back foot and to pitch the ball up and use the seam. I was being judged purely on the fact that I could play cricket, not whether I was coloured brown, purple, green or black.

Yet the old ambitions were still gnawing away at me. I reached 1,000 runs in that second season, more than Sobers again, although his average was better. I was hungry for cricket and I'd stop and watch any game, in case I could learn something. I was beginning to spread my cricketing wings as well – Cec Pepper, that fine Australian player who later became a first-class umpire, used to take sides all round the north and I'd play Sunday matches with giants like Gary Sobers, Wes Hall, Sonny Ramadhin and my old friend, Roy Gilchrist. I also played in a benefit match for Brian Statham at Didsbury and had the honour of changing in the same dressing room with men like Len Hutton, Denis Compton and Learie Constantine. They were wonderful to me, absolute gentlemen; they encouraged me, they praised me and handed on tips. They told me I was wrong to assume I'd gone as far in the game as I could expect. Were they right? Surely men like Hutton knew what they were talking about? But surely, too, I was already too old, with too many rough edges? But the thought kept nagging – wouldn't it be lovely to test myself against county cricketers, six hours a day, six days a week? Just one chance, and then I'd be happy at least to have tried to do my best.

Enter Ron Roberts. He was the kindest of men and a cricket fanatic with a wonderful relationship with players of all abilities, ages and colours. Ron was a gifted freelance cricket writer who used to take sides on winter tours to play good quality cricket in faraway places. He died in 1965 of a brain tumour before he was 40 and I'm just one of the many who still miss his genial encouragement of the lesser players on those tours where the great cricketers were just part of the team with no extra status. Anyway Ron asked me to go out to Rhodesia with his side in the first few months of 1962. I jumped at the chance and when I heard who else was in the party, I thought, 'If I don't learn anything from that lot, I don't deserve to play cricket for anyone.' Just listen to this gallery of talent – Ray Lindwall, Everton Weekes, Hanif Mohammad, Bobby Simpson, Sonny Ramadhin, Rohan Kanhai and Tom Graveney. It was the first time I'd met Tom Graveney, a man who was to have a profound influence on my life.

Ron, as a shrewd journalist, knew that there could be a few tense moments in Rhodesia because of the black players in his tour party. Before he left, he said to everyone, 'Now if anything happens out there that makes you want to pull out of the tour, I shall back you. But I hope we can all stick together.' A lot of the players asked me about the kind of things we would encounter. I told them about the signs that say, 'the right of admission is reserved' and that we had to be careful to avoid incidents at such times. But we couldn't really avoid trouble on occasions – there was the time when we were on our way from Salisbury to Bulawayo. In the leading car were Ron Roberts, Tom Graveney and Everton Weekes and the next contained Sonny Ramadhin, Ferge Gupte and myself. We stopped for a drink and I said to our lads, 'Stop here for five minutes and just wait to see if anything happens inside.' Within a couple of minutes, Tom came storming out and the first car drove off. 'What do you think has happened?' asked Sonny and Ferge, a West Indian and an Indian respectively. 'I know what's happened,' I told them grimly and Tom confirmed my suspicions later. Apparently, Tom ordered three gin and tonics but the barman refused to serve the West Indian, Everton Weekes. Tom was extremely upset, even though Everton was very gracious about it. Anyway, Everton got his own back when we arrived at Bulawayo; blacks and Coloureds weren't allowed to play on the best ground, so the game had to be played on a bumpy pitch with a hastily cut wicket. Everton knew about this and at a party that night, he was approached by a well-meaning bloke who said, 'I hope we'll see a first-class hundred from you tomorrow,' to which

Everton replied. 'If you give me a second-class ground to play on, then you'll get a second-class innings.' The next day, Everton went in and, almost immediately, he hit the ball straight up in the air and didn't wait to see the catch taken.

Then two West Indians, Rohan Kanhai and Chester Watson, were refused entry to a cocktail bar in an hotel. They complained and so did Ron Roberts to the hotel manager. Then the next morning, Sonny Ramadhin couldn't get his hair cut in the hotel's hairdressing salon. By this time, it was getting laughable, so Rohan decided to see the funny side of it and called off his decision to fly back home. But it was a close thing.

But back to the cricket and a match when I decided I'd had enough of all that idolatry surrounding the great players while I was known to hardly a soul. No offence to those marvellous cricketers I was with on that trip but I suddenly realized I would get nowhere near their standards unless I asserted myself and made the crowds take notice. The game was at Nairobi and I was getting fed up with all the spectators chatting about Graveney and co. Every time one of our batsmen was out, the spectators would all rush to the bar to refill their drinks and be ready for the next great exhibition of batting. I was sitting there with my pads on, moodily thinking, 'I bet they won't rush back from the bar when I'm walking in to bat' when Tom Graveney was out. I strode out, thinking, 'I'll make you lot watch me'. I was never so determined to put on a show and it was that attitude that lifted my standards that day. I smashed a century in 60 minutes and the second 50 came in just 19 minutes. I did it deliberately to get noticed and felt very proud as I walked off – and I felt even better as I looked up to see all my illustrious team-mates applauding. Five years later, I met up with Everton Weekes in Barbados where I was playing for the Rest of the World and he paid me the greatest compliment I've ever had. 'You know Bas,' he said, 'that knock at Nairobi was one of the finest I've ever seen and as I watched it, I thought you'd become a great player.'

Everton broadened my education in another way on that tour of Rhodesia – he made me take my first drink. I'd always hated the stuff and couldn't see why athletes should ruin their careers by forcing the stuff down their throats. I was brought up in a strict, Roman Catholic household in Cape Town, where there was no need for drink, and I never wanted one. Anyway, Everton came to me and said, 'Today is my 37th birthday and you are going to have a drink with me tonight, because nobody who is friends with me goes without a drink on my birthday.' Ray Lindwall was barman and he said, 'I'll take care of you Bas, leave it all to me. What would you like? I thought of the only drink I'd heard of and said, 'Gin and tonic.' Within an hour, after three drinks, I was being carted off to bed! It wasn't until I started playing at Worcester that I ever bothered with drink again and then, for some reason, it began to taste rather nice. I blame it all on cricket's social life, though.

That tour of Rhodesia was a crucial time for me; I wasn't disgraced in the company of so many class cricketers. At the end of the tour, the rest of the team presented me with a tankard inscribed, 'From the Boys.' I'd been accepted as an equal at last. I was beginning to relax in the company of cricketers.

Soon I became a sort of professional tourist – the following winter there was another Ron Roberts trip, this time to the Far East as well as Rhodesia and in 1963/4 I went to Pakistan with Alf Gover. On that tour of Rhodesia in the early months of 1963 something happened that smoothed my progress to the England team. We left Nairobi to fly to the Far East and we were scheduled to stop over in Bombay for just one night. We'd been in the field all day under a boiling hot sun and we were out on our feet by the time we arrived at Bombay airport. But the officials wouldn't let us into the country because I had a South African passport. 'But I'm a Coloured South African' I pleaded, 'I've got nothing to do with the apartheid regime. Just let me have a bed for the night, will you?' We found a compromise – I wrote down that I was South African by Indian parentage and I also had to find £200 to put down as a guarantee that I'd leave the next morning. So all the lads clubbed together and raised the cash and at last we got to bed! Later that year, when I joined Alf Gover's side to tour Pakistan, I told Alf about that problem and he suggested I took out a British passport. It seemed a sensible idea at the time and I didn't think I was being disloyal to my people in Cape Town. Little did I realize that this British passport would help clear the way to my selection for England in just over a couple more years.

During the summer of 1963, things were going well with Middleton. Everything in the garden was rosy but I still hankered for county cricket, especially after my encouraging performances on the Ron Roberts tours. I started playing in the 'Rothmans Cavaliers' games on Sundays and I enjoyed mixing with household names in these matches that were sponsored by the tobacco firm and were to prove the forerunner to the John Player League. Tom Graveney started chipping away at me to try for county cricket and his skipper at Worcester, Don Kenyon, told me he would put in a good word for me. But really my heart was in Lancashire. The folk up there had been so good to me that I would dearly have loved to turn out for their county at Old Trafford. John Kay, who was still on hand to offer guidance and encouragement, said he'd find out the lie of the land at Old Trafford. I was very excited at the prospect of staying in the Manchester area and I was disappointed when I received a letter from Lancashire's secretary, Geoffrey Howard, which extinguished my hopes. The county had just signed Sonny Ramadhin and Mr Howard said another overseas player would restrict the opportunities for younger, home grown players. Fair enough and I could understand that, but shortly afterwards I heard another reason for the decision. Cyril Washbrook, a great batsman in his day, was then an important man at Old Trafford, even though his playing days were over. Apparently, he was sent to run the rule over me and reported back that I was 'just a Saturday afternoon slogger' and that I wouldn't be a good signing. Well, he's entitled to his opinion, but fifteen years later, I was particularly delighted to receive one of my six Gillette Cup Man of the Match Awards from the adjudicator, none other than Cyril Washbrook.

By the time I'd gone to Pakistan with Alf Gover's side I was beginning to get cold feet about playing county cricket, despite the tempting offers that came my way from several counties. Was I over-reaching myself again? Was I too old? Was I good enough? I was sitting with Tom Graveney in the Hotel Metropole in Karachi, confiding in him about my fears when he said, 'I'm fed up with all this talk about you not being good enough. I'm telling you that there's no reason why you can't play for England if you start playing county cricket next season.' I was astonished at his confidence in me; I don't know whether it was just blarney to boost my ego but such words from a man like Graveney would make anyone think he could play the game. I told him about the counties who were interested in me and he was fair enough to say that the county he'd recently left after a bitter dispute – Gloucestershire – would do me very nicely because they would treat me well. 'But I'd really like you to come to Worcester,' he said. 'You could help us win a few trophies.' Of course, I was flattered by his remarks and the fact that I already knew several of the Worcestershire players helped me make up my mind. The negotiations with the Worcestershire committee were very civilized and I was also very impressed with the attitude of the Middleton club. I was just about to sign another three-year contract with Middleton but as soon as they heard why I wanted to leave they were delighted. In the absence of a concrete offer from Lancashire, I just had to leave that cosy little town where I'd been so happy and try my luck in Worcester.

A couple of years later, I heard the truth behind Middleton's offer to join them as their professional in 1960 – and it convinced me that someone up above looks after me. After Roy Gilchrist had announced he was leaving Middleton, the club searched around for a replacement in the same fiery, fast bowling mould. They had settled terms with Wes Hall, who was on his way to becoming a great quickie; but Wes asked them to keep quiet about it until the start of the 1960 season. He had a good job with a brewery back in Barbados and he didn't want them to find out he'd be off playing cricket in Lancashire from April to September the following year. Somehow the truth leaked out, the firm put pressure on Wes and he had to cancel his contract with Middleton in February. That's why Middleton were so keen to take me on – they had had so little time left to find someone that they thought they would take a chance on me. At that late stage all the clubs had fixed up their pros – a fact confirmed to me by John Arlot. So if somebody hadn't blabbed about how Wes Hall was planning to spend a few months in England, I wouldn't be sitting here in my pleasant semi-detached in Worcester, looking back on a career that owes a hell of a lot to fate.

3 Learning the Ropes at Worcester

I went to Worcester determined to do two things: to make the grade in county cricket and to cover up my age. As far as I was concerned the two were inter-connected, because if Worcestershire had discovered how old I *really* was, I don't believe they would have offered me a contract. In the Coloured communities of South Africa, things like birth certificates aren't that important. You can go several years before being registered and, often, things get slightly twisted. That's where I was lucky. I told everyone I was born in 1934 which made me 29 years and six months when I first played for Worcestershire. A few years later, after I'd proved myself in first-class cricket and established a reasonable Test Match career, I lopped another three years off my year of birth, making it 1931. And that's where it's staying, although I can assure you I'm a little older than my birth certificate states – but not much! If you told me I was nearer forty than 35 when I first played for England in 1966, I wouldn't sue you for slander.

No matter how old I was, I was determined enough when I joined Worcestershire in 1964 – and what I overheard in the nets made me even more ambitious. I was trying to come to terms with the wealth of bowlers and the grass practice wickets when I overheard one of the first-team say, 'he'll never make it, not the way he plays'. I suppose it was fair comment but it just made me buckle down. I pretended I hadn't heard but inwardly I thought, 'I'll show you lot.' I practised every hour I could, even getting Naomi and Damian to bowl a few balls at me in the back garden to keep the flow of batting going in my body. Just as I had tried to topple Sobers from his pinnacle in my early days in the Central Lancashire League, now I set my stall out to reach an established player's standard. That man was Tom Graveney. I know that sounds ridiculous, considering the vast gap between our respective batting skills, but I had to keep aiming high to make up for lost time. Within a couple of years I would be one of the oldest players in this side, even though I would have managed just a couple of seasons in county cricket. Time was not on my side, so I had to cram everything into a very short period. I told Tom I was going to be as good a batsman as him and he smiled. 'Forget it, Bas, you'll never be as good as me for all sorts of reasons that aren't your fault.' But I told him I would keep trying to topple him and I think our friendly rivalry kept him on his toes during our time together at Worcester.

In 1964, Worcester had a fine side. They won the county championship that year with a blend that included seven England players. That just underlined how much I had to do if I was to get a regular place in the side for the following season after I'd completed my year of qualification for the county. Watching the players in the nets, I realized I had to tighten up all round. The bowlers didn't bowl loosely even in the nets, and the batsman had to work hard at his game. After my initial spell of disappointment with Middleton, I'd worked out a line of attack that enabled me to pick up quick runs at the start of my innings. Not any more. Now I had to discipline myself, to wait for the rare loose delivery and then capitalize on it. I watched how Tom Graveney played the fast bowlers – placing his front foot down the wicket and playing the ball down with masterly control. I realized I lacked the skill and the height to do that, so I looked at Don Kenyon's method. Don Kenyon was the man who always seemed to figure in the cricket scores I read back home. At the age of 40, he was still a master of fast and seam bowling. I realized the English first-game revolved round seam bowling so I thought: 'Kenyon's been a top opening batsman for 20 years, he's the man to watch when I want to play the seamers.' I noticed he played all the quick bowlers from the back foot because it gave him that split second extra to make a late adjustment against a ball that could be swinging all over the place. That was good enough for me, especially as I'd always been a back foot player.

I realized I also had to do something about my bowling. There was no point in developing my off-spin with an England all-rounder, Martin Horton, in the side to give balance with his batting and his off-breaks. I reasoned that seam bowling might make me valuable to the team because the English conditions helped me swing and cut the ball, so I knuckled down to watching Jack Flavell and Len Coldwell, those fine opening bowlers who both played for England. Although I could bowl seamers, I wasn't accurate enough so I stood directly behind Flavell and noticed how near he got to the stumps without touching them. His arm would come down dead straight, in line with the stumps at the other end. That's why he bowled so straight. I also learned much about the theory of swing bowling from Len Coldwell, a lovely, easy-going bloke. He would sit and think out his batsmen by working out exactly where he would bowl his huge inswingers to a particular player. He would know when to bowl straight at the stumps and when to use the extreme end of the bowling crease. In their contrasting ways, Flavell and Coldwell helped me to develop my bowling and also to realize how much brainpower and technique I'd have to face every day in county cricket.

I started to acquire even more mental toughness, a quality I felt I had always had as a player. But now I was in a hard professional school where runs and averages meant jobs to some players. I would never play for my average and it used to amaze me that some bowlers or batsmen knew exactly how they'd fared as they came off the field at the close of play. But it was a job of work to many of them and their whole livelihood depended on statistical success. I thought a lot about my technique but apart from a conscious decision to play off the back foot, I don't think I altered my style all that radically. I certainly didn't alter the way I attacked the ball and I continued to hit the ball through the covers with all the power and control coming from my right hand. That was something that amazed Ron Roberts when I toured with him. 'Tell me, Bas,' he said, 'how do you hit the ball through the covers without your left hand doing the work?' I couldn't answer him, I wasn't aware I was doing anything wrong, and I decided not to change that style just because it wasn't approved by the text book. One thing that was in my favour as I began to play county cricket was the fact that I played very late, with a low backlift, so that I could usually work the ball away for a single to keep the scoreboard moving. It was a far cry from my days on Signal Hill where I'd try to hit every ball into the sea!

I wanted to look nice with the bat, to be a classical player in the Cowdrey and Graveney mould. I'd sit with my pads on and listen to the spectators say, 'Oh, what a lovely shot from Graveney!' and I'd wish they could say the same about me. But I was never a purist and I had to make up for that deficiency in other ways – like the ability to punish the bad ball. I realized there was no shame in battling to keep out the good deliveries but it was unprofessional not to profit from any loose stuff that came along. Then I would hit the ball with brute force. I evolved the shape of an innings; I'd give the first hour to the bowler, get settled in and become accustomed to the light and the bounce of the wicket. Then I would step up the tempo and aim for a $3\frac{1}{2}$-hour hundred by punishing the bowlers I'd blocked earlier in my innings.

Because I had to qualify for a year before I could play in the county championship, I had to make do with occasional non-championship appearances and Second XI matches, and I also turned out for Kidderminster in the Birmingham League. It was a frustrating period for me. I'd made my decision to try to play county cricket and I felt irritated that I had to make do with second-class cricket. No offence meant to the very friendly lads I played with at Kidderminster, particularly Peter Harris, the genial skipper, but I was wishing the season away. I felt that the longer I stayed in second-class cricket, the more difficult it would be to reach a higher standard. There was no lack of ability in the Birmingham League, it was just that I missed the intense atmosphere of the Central Lancashire League where everything was so much more competitive.

Fortunately, help was at hand and it came in the shape of a well-timed boot up the D'Oliveira bottom. Charlie Hallows was a fine batsman with Lancashire and at that time he was the coach at Worcester. After a few weeks, he took me to one side and said, 'I was one of the main instigators in getting you here and you're disappointing me. You're not playing to your full potential and if you think you're going to walk into the First XI next season, you're wrong. You've got to battle and do yourself justice.' It scared me stiff and I managed to score a couple of hundreds for the Second XI in the following week. Charlie then came to me and said, 'Now that makes it easier for everybody because you've shown you can play a bit.' He was right and today I say the same things to players on the fringe of the First XI – if you want to get on in cricket, you've got to learn your trade in the seconds, you've got to graft away in front of two men and a dog. When you walk to the wicket, tell yourself you're going to get a hundred, or if you're bowling that you can't afford to let the dollies block you.'

I've always thought that if you stay in the Second XI too long, the edge goes off your cricket. The whole environment of first-class cricket is so different, not least of all when it comes to concentration. That's something I've always enjoyed; I'd sit and watch the game for hours and pick out certain things to apply for myself when it became my turn to get involved. In that first season at Worcester, I watched as much first-class cricket as I could. I tried to work out when a batsman started to take control of things, how he found the gaps, which bowlers kept on running in with optimism and fire, even though they were being smashed. I made notes about the bowlers because I wanted to be aware of their defects as well as their strengths when it came to be my turn to face them. The subtle field-placings fascinated me – the way a fielder would be moved a yard either side of his original position when a new batsman came in, because they had heard about a particular weakness. All these players seemed to know so much more about cricket than I did. But at least I felt mentally equipped for first-class cricket because I'd been doing my homework meticulously. Time would tell if I was a good enough player.

My first taste of the big-time came against the Australians under Bobby Simpson's captaincy. I batted at number six and I loved the power, the aggression, the sheer dynamism of the Aussies; they wanted to roll you over and it was up to you to stand in their way. I didn't score very many but one thing sticks in my mind from that match. Off the last ball before tea I cut an off-spinner from Tom Veivers behind point for a couple of runs. I walked off, slightly annoyed that I hadn't put it properly when I heard one of the Aussie players say, 'Fancy playing that bloody shot just before tea!' I was amazed because as far as I was concerned, a loose ball is there to be punished, whatever the time of the day. You can't hang around waiting for the loose delivery, only to block it because it's near an interval. I carried that philosophy through all my playing

career and whenever I got myself out to a bad shot I was the
first to acknowledge it. But I also scored a few runs by hammering the loose delivery.

I met up with the Australians again at the end of that
season when I got a hundred off them in a carefree Festival
match at Hastings. It was a lovely wicket, the Aussies were
tired and wanted to go home, so I didn't attach much impor-
tance to my knock. But I understand it made big headlines in
South Africa. So that was the end of my first season in first-
class cricket; I'd only had eight innings and I was hungry for
more. But first I had to work out how I was going to get
permanently into a side that had just won the county championship for the first time. I still had a lot of work to do and I
started looking at the men I would have to displace. It couldn't
be the top three batsmen, Kenyon, Horton and Graveney. Ron
Headley and Dick Richardson were not only fine stroke-
makers but also splendid close-to-the-wicket fielders. There
was no point in aiming for their places so I settled on Jim
Standen. Now Jim was a fine seamer – he finished top of the
averages in 1964 – but I was a better batsman. I thought that if
I could develop my seam bowling I might get in the side ahead
of him on merit. It was nothing personal, but I had to set my
targets and try to reach them, otherwise I'd just be kicking my
heels in the seconds. In the end I managed it and took Jim's
place. I also fancied standing at first slip but Dick Richardson
was already there; but I went all out to get that spot because I
thought I could do it and that Dick was such a magnificent
fielder anywhere that the side wouldn't suffer. I can see why
Dick was annoyed – it seemed as if I got in and batted
where I wanted, I fielded and bowled when I wished. It was the
first time that I'd experienced tension of the sort that stems
from a team-mate being annoyed that he has to make way for
someone else. I could understand the irritation of both Jim and
Dick but in the end, I thought, 'Well, I'm here now and
nobody's going to dislodge me if I have anything to do with
it.' Eventually Dick and I became firm friends and I never
blamed him at all for his attitude, which was completely professional. That's one of the reasons why that Worcestershire
side was such a good one – we had competition breathing
down our necks.

I began the 1965 season in the first team and our first championship match was at Worcester against Essex. I desperately wanted to do well – I did and I scored 108. It was an immensely satisfying innings because I implemented many of the principles I'd filed away in my brain during the previous season. The conditions were all against the batsmen as I walked down the steps to bat; it was dark, spitting with rain and bitterly cold. 'This is it,' I kept saying as I walked slowly out to the wicket, 'whatever happens, this is the big one for you.' I was very nervous and was glad Tom Graveney was out there to encourage me. The ball was seaming about all over the place and we were up against two fine bowlers – Trevor Bailey, not so quick in those days but who still had it all upstairs, and Barry Knight, a man good enough to play against Australia in the following winter. I just hung on, telling myself things would get better, trying to reassure myself that if I could make it on this wicket, I was in clover for the rest of my career. Things got easier in the afternoon and when Knight took the new ball, I paid him back for some of my traumas in the morning by hitting him straight back over his head for six. I'll never forget the curious sidelong glance Barry gave me as that ball sailed away.

That night, I was exhilarated and flattered at all the praise. I was particularly pleased that my method of building an innings had worked and I vowed to stick to it whenever possible. That's why I was usually one of the slowest batsmen in first-class cricket in my first hour! So I'd picked up a century on a bowlers' paradise and the whole thing was immensely satisfying. Perhaps I could play this game after all. The following week, one of those quirks of the fixture calendar found us playing Essex again in the county championship. This time it was at Brentwood on a turning wicket against the spin of Robin Hobbs and Paddy Phelan. I made 163 and my pleasure at getting a hundred on a seamers' wicket one week and another on a spinners' wicket shortly afterwards was magnified when Don Kenyon awarded me with my county cap as I walked off the field. That frustrating year of 1964 seemed a million years away now as I started to consolidate a place in the Worcestershire side on merit.

Things went fantastically well for me in that season. We

won the county championship and Tom Graveney and I were
the only two batsmen to reach 1,500 runs in the county
championship. I also picked up a few wickets – and my first
99 in first-class cricket! I remember vividly the day we
retained the title. We were playing at Hove and we scraped
home by just a few wickets. I was given out LBW and
couldn't bear to watch then, so I sat in the dressing room. As
Roy Booth and Dick Richardson brought us nearer to victory,
I tried to get out and have a look but Joe Lister, our secretary,
kept saying, 'Stay where you are, don't change the pattern, it'll
bring us bad luck!' I never saw the winning run, just heard the
cheers, and then we settled down to a hell of a party. Dick
Richardson and I ended up with some of the local police at
Hove and at one stage we were all set to sleep on Brighton
beach – but Dick eventually decided to drive us back and
Naomi, who wasn't expecting me back that night got the
shock of her life when I walked in in the small hours.

I think that 1965 Worcestershire side was the best one I've
played in. We had tremendous bowling strength with four
men – Flavell, Coldwell, Gifford and Horton – who had each
taken 100 wickets in a season. The fielding was good – Headley and Richardson particularly – and the batting was solid
and attractive. And we had in Roy Booth a canny wicket-
keeper who made few mistakes and who could always nick a
few vital runs with the bat. I was so lucky to come into a side
with such experience and professionalism; I just had to learn
something from them. I concentrated like mad in that first full
season and I was exhausted at the end; so much so that I didn't
take any notice of the newspaper talk that I had just missed out
on the trip to Australia with Mike Smith's England side. I dis-
counted that idea straight away – me, a coloured South African, playing for England? The significance of Alf Gover's
advice about my passport hadn't yet dawned on me and
besides, I was certain I wasn't anywhere good enough. I
looked at the batsmen selected to tour – Boycott, Edrich,
Barber, Cowdrey, Smith, Parks, Russell and Barrington – and
realized I had no right to consider myself in their class.

At the end of that season, with the champagne corks pop-
ping at Hove, Len Coldwell summed it all up for me – 'We
win the championship, you score all these runs and get wickets

as well . . . all in your first year. What more can you hope for?' I wanted nothing else. I had proved myself at the highest level I thought I could reach.

4 Playing for England

In 1966 I achieved something I shall be proud of till my dying day – I played for England, the country that gave me a chance denied to me by the land of my birth. But I played for England under false pretences. I wasn't fit enough. Yet playing for Test cricket meant so much to me that I deliberately kept my shoulder injury a secret.

It all started one December night in 1965 when I was injured in a car crash near Worcester. One of the other passengers was killed, so I was one of the lucky ones, even though I didn't think so at the time. My right shoulder was badly damaged and surgeons weren't sure if I could play again. I couldn't lift my right arm for several weeks and I nearly despaired at the thought of missing a season and having to start learning my trade all over again – or, even worse, of packing up cricket just when I was making some progress.

Worcestershire were due to go on tour to Jamaica in March and I went to the indoor nets to test out my shoulder. It was hopeless – I couldn't bowl or throw. Bill Powell, the club masseur, worked wonders and got me into some kind of shape and I made the tour. My skipper, Don Kenyon, bowled me straight through for 25 overs on the trot in the first match. I felt no reaction and I could bat freely as well. But I couldn't throw, all I could manage was an underhand flip. It stayed that way for another year. Only my Worcestershire team-mates knew the extent of my injury. The selectors didn't know and even though Don Kenyon was one of them, he didn't let on, otherwise they would never have picked a man for a five-day Test who couldn't throw the ball! The press never found out either; what a story that would have made for them. It's amazing to recall but I never once had to throw during that season. I fielded at slip all the time and whenever I had to run for the ball, there was either an easy single or two involved and I was never tested. I know I was morally in the wrong, but once I'd been selected for England, nothing was going to stop me from winning a cap. But a man who can't throw is a liability in a

Test and I should have reported myself unfit. I must be honest though – I'd do the same again, because appearing for England was simply an unbelievable experience for me . . . if I'd dropped out, I probably would have missed my chance because I was only ever going to be a stop-gap on the grounds of age and ability.

In 1966 I carried on where I'd left off the previous season. Things were going well, both with bat and ball, but I was unprepared for the events of Sunday, May 29th. I was playing at Beaconsfield in Buckinghamshire in a benefit game for my team-mate Martin Horton. I was batting with Ron Headley when a loudspeaker announcement said that the team for the First Test had been released. The players all stopped to listen and Ron Headley said, 'I'll bet you a pound you're in the twelve.' I was genuinely astonished at his suggestion and said, 'You're on, you must be mad.' The last name to be read out was mine. It was unreal – who were these blokes crowding round to congratulate me? Why were all those spectators clapping me? I wasn't English, I was a Coloured South African, yet I was to play for England just six years after leaving Cape Town. I immediately thought of all the people I'd known, all those who'd helped me or been nice to me in that time. But then I came back to earth and realised I ought to phone Naomi. I thrashed around with the bat , got a quick hundred and dialled home. I said, 'Have you heard?'; came the down-to-earth reply, 'Heard what?'. I didn't realize that Naomi wouldn't have been listening to the radio. 'I've been picked for England.' The phone went dead for fully a minute and I thought we'd been cut off – 'are you there, Naomi?' I said, and then I realized she was crying. Eventually she said, 'Ring me later, because I can't take this now.' I felt the same way as her.

What a great night we had! Jugs and jugs of beer and plenty of songs and cheering. I couldn't believe that people could be so happy for just one person. Apart from the nagging problems of conscience about my shoulder injury (and I knew I couldn't possibly play the boy scout and own up), those next few days were blissfully happy. Affection from the British public came out loud and clear – from phone calls, by post, in the pubs and when I walked down the street. Strangers would come up and say, 'Well done, we're proud of you.' Why did I appeal to so many people who knew nothing about cricket? I suppose it was because they realized what I'd come through. Their sincerity deeply touched me.

So I went up to Old Trafford, loving all the public attention. I felt very sheepish in the presence of the experienced English players. Colin Cowdrey introduced himself to me – we'd never met even though we were to be in the same side! A lot of the lads from Middleton came to see me at the ground and I felt so pleased for their wonderful club. One of them said to me, 'Do you know, Bas, we never thought you'd make it at Worcester, never mind England – we're so pleased we were wrong.' I can understand their doubts; nobody who had seen me playing three years earlier in the League could possibly have tipped me as an England player, especially at my age. What the hell was I doing here?

On the eve of the match I went to look at the wicket and noticed there was a lot of grass on it. I was rooming with that shrewd Gloucestershire off-spinner, David Allen, and I asked him who he thought would drop out the next day. He said, 'If that same amount of grass is on the wicket tomorrow morning, then you'll play. If they shave it off, I imagine I'll be in the side.' I never slept a wink that night as I turned the events of the last six years over in my mind. The next morning, the grass had been shaved and David Allen played – the correct decision because the ball started turning on the second day. I was in the nets when the England skipper, Mike Smith, walked past me and said in that amiably low-key way of his, 'Will you do twelfth man, please, Bas?' I said 'Fine, captain.' I wasn't disappointed, I swear it. Just being part of a Test was a miracle for me. I sat on the balcony when England went out to field and I looked along at the blokes sitting beside me – Doug Insole, Peter May, Don Kenyon and Alec Bedser. The England selectors and there I was sitting with them, watching a Test! Ten years previously I'd watched Insole and May in a Test at Cape Town; I'd seen Peter May bang the ball over the top time after time and wondered what it would be like to have the same gifts as that great batsman. Yet now here he was, sitting beside me, with a high enough opinion of my ability to select me for England. Unbelievable.

I saw the first two days of the Old Trafford Test before I returned to play for Worcestershire on the Saturday. Gary Sobers played such a magnificent knock on the first day that the old doubts kept recurring: Basil D'Oliveira, look out there and see a true Test batsman smashing the England attack. Now what right have you got to be on the same pitch as a man like that? Quite so. On reflection, though, it was a good Test in which to be twelfth man, because England lost by an innings on a wicket tailor-made for Lance Gibbs' off-spin. If I had played, I would have had to bowl on a beautiful wicket after Sobers had won the toss and then, when it came to my turn to bat, the ball would have been turning square. It could have been the end of my Test career and there would have been no complaints from me. When I left the team on Friday night to return to Worcester they all made a point of coming up to me, saying 'cheerio, see you again'. I thought, 'perhaps they know something I don't', and so I remained fairly optimistic I'd get my chance, especially as the game was such a resounding defeat. Well, that chance came in the next Test; four men were dropped, including the captain, Mike Smith. Colin Cowdrey took over and I was going to play my first Test at, of all places, Lord's.

Lord's meant everything to me. I'd read so much about that place – grounds like Melbourne, Sydney, Barbados, Bombay and Johannesburg could never have the same effect as Lord's does on a cricketer. Don't ask me why, but I guess it's a combination of mystique, tradition and atmosphere. I'd been there once before as a spectator – in 1963 in that famous drawn Test against the West Indies when Colin Cowdrey came in with his broken arm to defy Wes Hall in the last over. Now, just three years later, I was to play for England under Colin Cowdrey's captaincy against Wes Hall! I got to the ground very early that first morning, before any of the players. Colin Cowdrey had already told me I was in the side and I wanted to savour every moment of the day. I stood on the player's balcony at about half-past nine and thought, 'I wish they could see me at Signal Hill now.' It was then that I suddenly realized this Test Match was for my own people, not for me. I thought about the conditions under which I'd learned my cricket, I thought about John Arlott, the lads from Middle-

11 The prodigal son returns home – and the welcome from these boys touched and gratified me.

12 May 1966 at Beaconsfield, Bucks – on the day I was first picked for England, I lead the Worcestershire side off the field. One of the greatest days of my life.

13 Twelfth man for England – Old Trafford, 1966 against the West Indies.
Back row, left to right
– Russell, Jones, Brown, Higgs, Milburn, myself.
Front row,
left to right
– Parks, Titmus, Smith, Cowdrey, Barrington and Allen.

14 and **15** Checking out the ball skills of my eldest son, Damian and his little brother, Shaun. Fifteen years later, and they've changed a little. Damian is the one with the moustache first popularized by his old man.

16 Touring West Indies with the England team, 1967/8. My three great friends Rohan Kanhai (left), Wes Hall and Seymour Nurse. They weren't bad cricketers, either.

17 An unusual team group of the England party in the West Indies, 1967/8.

18 My great friend, Tom Graveney, leads out the tourists in the game against Barbados, 1968. From left to right, Alan Knott, Jim Parks, myself, Graveney, Pat Pocock and John Edrich.

19 The Fifth Test Match against Australia at the Oval in August 1968 – on my way to a century which would be memorable in more ways than one.

ton but above all, my humble gratitude and affection that morning was for Benny Bansda and the folk of Signal Hill. As the telegrams poured in that morning, I thought, 'Please God, let me do well – I shan't ask for anything else. I'd hate to let everyone down.'

It rained at the start and although we didn't begin on time, we had announced our side and I was in. Ken Barrington realized how much it all meant to me, even though we were sitting kicking our heels, waiting for the rain to relent. 'Whatever happens now, Bas, they can't take it away from you', he said. 'You've been picked and you'll be able to keep your England cap and sweater for evermore.' That night, I took my England cap to my room and slept with it just a few feet away from me. From that day on, I considered everything else a bonus. And when I was introduced to the Queen on Monday, it was too much for me. As I stood in line, I kept thinking, 'What shall I say if she speaks to me?' Well, sure enough, she did – and I haven't a clue what she said or what I mumbled in reply.

It was a great game of cricket. It was the match in which the great partnership of Sobers and Holford saved the game for the West Indies. It ended with England 87 short of victory with six wickets in hand after Colin Milburn had scored a typically swashbuckling century. And it was the Test when Tom Graveney celebrated his return to the England side, after an absence of three years, with 96; he was furious with himself for getting out, caught at the wicket, trying to run the ball down through the slips. I think he felt he owed a century to all the selectors of the past who hadn't picked him and settled for batsmen with just a fraction of his talent. Tom's successful return to Test cricket in that match was one of the happiest memories of a thrilling experience.

I was quite pleased with my own performance as well. At the start of the match, I stood at slip and just listened to the words of wisdom from Cowdrey, Titmus and wicket-keeper Parks. What could a novice like me have to offer in tactical terms? I picked up my first Test wicket fairly quickly and it was quite a scalp – that fine player, Seymour Nurse. It wasn't due to any high quality bowling from me, he simply misjudged the line and I bowled him round his legs with an outswinger that came back into the leg stump. I didn't know much in those days about making the ball go where I wanted and I certainly didn't intend this dismissal – but it pinged out Nurse's leg-stump and it looked a great picture in next morning's papers!

But my real test of temperament came on the Saturday when I batted for England for the first time. I was terribly nervous, in the same state of mind as when I first batted for Middleton and Worcestershire – but the reception I got from the crowd was unbelievable as I walked out. What is it about the English that makes them take to one person and not to another of equal merit? Perhaps the crows on that warm Saturday were cheering the underdog, in the way only the English can. My mind was in a complete turmoil as I passed Colin Cowdrey on the way to the wicket. It seemed to take an eternity to get past the members in the Long Room on the way out to bat, but once I set foot on the grass, it felt just like any other match. Gary Sobers was bowling with the new ball, always a dangerous time for the right-hand batsman, because he had to guard against the Sobers ball that nipped back into him, as well as the one that moved away towards the slips. Because of our duels in the Central Lancashire League, there was always a spot of tension on the field between Gary and myself – and this was no exception. His second ball nearly had me; I nicked the outswinger, but kept the handle well down and although David Allan, the wicket-keeper, dived forward and got a glove to the ball, he couldn't hold it. From then on, everything went smoothly; I followed my usual precept of settling in slowly and carefully before launching an offensive and one early clip off my toes for a boundary off Charlie Griffith put me in great heart. I was going well, I could sense the crowd was behind me and at the other end, Jim Parks was playing well. We had put on 48 when Jim drove a Wes Hall half-volley straight back. I couldn't get out of the way and the ball hit my right heel, then on to my stumps. Wes and I both stopped as if to say, 'Is that out or not?' Of course, it wasn't but we were both momentarily frozen in thought. Wes reacted better than I did and recovered in time to pick up the ball and whip out a stump. Wes said, 'Sorry, Bas' as I walked out and I kept my head down because I felt a fool for getting out like that. I was embarrassed and frustrated because I was playing well and loving the atmosphere. But I'll never forget the ovation I got from the crowd – for scoring just 27 runs! I thought, 'If that's what I get for 27 runs, I can't wait to make a Test hundred.'

At least I hadn't disgraced myself, apart from my ridiculous dismissal. That was the only innings I had in the match and I loved everything about that Test. But I wasn't prepared for the fatigue that settled over me when the game ended on the Tuesday night. I was absolutely done in. I'd been drained by the atmosphere, the tension, the people I'd met during those six days and I was in no state at all to play for Worcestershire the next day. I did play of course but I was still unwinding after the Test. After that, I used to pray that we didn't bat first whenever I returned from a Test, because those few hours in the field in the county game would help me unwind and shape my attitude for batting. I'd be okay after the first day back, but believe me, I had found the strain immense after that Lord's Test.

England lost the next Test at Trent Bridge by 139 runs. It was another classic example of the West Indies' ability to battle out of trouble. We led by 90 on the first innings – with Tom Graveney getting that belated century – but then they put the block on things and just occupied the crease for a few hours. It seemed odd to watch stroke-players like Butcher and Kanhai just sitting on the splice and I didn't blame them. Test cricket is a hard business and they had plenty of time to build up a large lead. They did – Butcher got a double hundred and they set us a target of 393 on a turning wicket. We didn't bat terribly well and that summed up the difference between the two sides.

My abiding memory of that match is a masterful 94 by Gary Sobers. It was the best innings I saw that summer; he just devastated us in a couple of hours after Kanhai and Butcher had worn us down. Eventually he gave it away, caught having a slog off Ken Higgs with never a thought for his hundred. That's the way Gary played the game.

I was pleased with my own form, scoring two half-centuries and helping Derek Underwood add 65 for the last wicket. I was feeling confident against the West Indians because they didn't like it when you attacked them. I noticed they seemed to bowl better when you allowed them to carry the fight to you. That was never my style – apart from that first hour of reconnaissance – and I enjoyed the challenge. I also enjoyed a spot of leg-pulling in that Test with Wes Hall. You may have gathered by now that Wes was one of my favourite cricketers; a superb fast bowler but a genuine sportsman through and through and also a very intelligent man. I remember when we thought he'd been caught out on our tour of Rhodesia with Ron Roberts. Willie Watson, our captain, was supposed to speak for the guests at a dinner but unfortunately he was a little indisposed and he called on Wes to do the honours. 'What me?' he said. 'What the hell can I say?' So he got up and said, 'I feel like the man who owned a harem. When he walked into this holy of holies and saw all these beautiful women, he said – I know what to do but I don't know where to start!' Well, that brought the house down and Wes gave a very witty, articulate speech. When it was time to meet up in Test Matches, we were always having a go at each other. When he came in to bat at Trent Bridge, I was standing at first slip and told him to play his beloved flick shot off his legs. He did and the stumps went flying. 'Just you wait till it's your turn,' he told me. So when I walked in, I got a couple of bouncers from big Wes and he called out, 'That's for the flick shot!' A great bloke and competitor.

I wasn't so fond of his opening partner, Charlie Griffith. Charlie was pleasant enough for most of the time but he was angry at reports that were branding him as a 'chucker'. Nobody ever called him for throwing in England and I can understand his anger at the innuendos. But that was no excuse for hitting Derek Underwood in the face with a bouncer. Derek was playing his first Test and was simply blocking out the bowlers as the match petered slowly to a victory for the tourists. The bouncer was uncalled for, Derek was the last man and there was no danger of England saving the match. Luckily, Derek recovered and even though Charlie wrote and apologized, it left a nasty taste in the England dressing room – and I know Gary Sobers wasn't happy either.

Charlie also behaved badly in the next Test at Leeds when Colin Cowdrey tried to get into the West Indies dressing room to get some autographs for bats. When Colin pushed the door open, Charlie was standing behind it and as soon as he saw the England captain, he shut the door in his face. I'm not sure whether he was annoyed at Colin in particular or whether he had it in for the whole England side. Certainly there was some needle in that Leeds Test, an atmosphere for which I was partly responsible.

The flashpoint happened on the Saturday, with England struggling to save the follow-on. The West Indies had made 500 for 9 and Wes Hall tore into our batting with the fastest spell of bowling I'd ever seen. He dismissed Boycott, hit Milburn such a blow on the elbow that he retired hurt, and beat Graveney and Cowdrey for sheer pace. It was a slow wicket but he was still five yards faster than John Snow, our quickest bowler that summer. When I came in to bat, Wes was still fiery but eventually he retired to the outfield after a truly magnificent match-winning spell of fast bowling. Ken Higgs and I started to retrieve the situation and the score advanced to 169 for 7, with my score 65. Then Lance Gibbs bowled to me and I tried to clip him over the top of mid-wicket. I didn't connect properly and I thought 'I'm out' as the ball sailed towards Conrad Hunte; but the ball dipped and Conrad had to dive forward to attempt the catch. He came up, claiming the catch and although I knew Conrad to be a scrupulously fair man, I felt he had misjudged the catch and taken the ball on the half-volley. I didn't think he was cheating, just that he had made an error of judgement. The two close fielders – Gary Sobers and Seymour Nurse – started applauding Conrad but they stopped when I refused to move from the crease. 'Aren't you walking?' said Gary. 'No, because he never caught it,' I said. Then Seymour said, 'Conrad isn't the kind of fellow to make a mistake like that.' By this time I was getting annoyed and said, 'Well, if he isn't, he's started now', to which Gary replied 'bloody hell' just after the umpire Charlie Elliott had given me 'not out'. That's when I really saw red and I got up from my guard and told Gary, 'Come off it, I've got a long memory, you know. I remember playing against you in Lancashire and we all thought you were caught twice behind the wicket. We thought you'd touched the ball but you weren't given out, so don't start complaining just because the umpire agrees with me.'

The bad atmosphere continued and I finally lost my temper, thinking, 'Right you lot, I'm going to smash you all out of sight.' Gary brought back Wes Hall and I hit him straight back over his head for a six, one of the finest shots I've ever played. I was savouring the crowd's applause when I looked up and saw Wes clapping me slowly, but looking straight back at me in an extremely menacing fashion. I thought he would bounce me after that, but in fact, he kept the ball well up and waited for me to get myself out. In my mood of pent-up anger, my end wasn't long a-coming. I tried to smash Griffith out of sight and skied one to the covers for 88.

I went straight to my captain Colin Cowdrey and apologized for my part in the incident. I'd just finished a shower when Peter May walked in. He asked for my side of the events – always one of his best characteristics was a readiness to listen to the other man's view – and then he said, 'Can I offer you a spot of advice? When you play this game, do so with cotton wool in your ears. Today you played beautifully, you did all the hard work. The ball was old, you had them on their knees, you should have scored 150 and we could have avoided the follow-on. But you lost your temper because you listened to people on the cricket field.' He was absolutely right – an angry bloke is half a man. I've never forgotten that priceless piece of advice.

Unfortunately, I was still annoyed at the West Indians, particularly when I heard that Conrad Hunte was the only one to applaud me back to the pavilion after I'd been dismissed on the Saturday. So when I batted again on the Monday, I didn't answer when some of them said, 'Good morning'. Now I know that was childish but I felt so bitter about them continuing the argument after Charlie Elliott had given me 'not out'. But the feud didn't last long – Gary had me caught round the corner off a magnificent slower ball and then the tail just folded up. We lost by an innings and plenty.

For the last Test at the Oval we had yet another captain, our third of the series. Brian Close was different from Smith and Cowdrey in that he didn't know how to defend. He would force things to happen on the field and, of course, he had a plan to get Sobers out cheaply. He told us John Snow would bounce him early on and that he expected Gary to have a go, simply because he was that kind of batsman. Sure enough it worked in their second innings. In came Sobers and tried to hook the first ball from Snow; he mishit, the ball flew off the under-edge of the bat on to his box, then up in the air to the safe hands of Close at short leg. A lesser man than Close would have ducked as soon as he saw Gary shape up for the hook – but he just stood his ground and waited for the mis-cue. That was the killer for the West Indies and they in turn folded up, giving us an innings victory.

A lot of people thought they eased up in that Oval Test because the series was already won. Don't you believe it. We were lucky, I agree – that every catch went to hand, that everything Close tried succeeded, that Tom Graveney and John Murray forged a magnificent partnership when we needed it, and that John Snow and Ken Higgs put on 128 for the last wicket against a tired attack. But you make your own luck to a certain extent and we played positively all the way through. I didn't even mind getting yorked by my old mate, Wes Hall – a beautiful delivery that exposed the deficiencies of my back-foot technique. Despite all my practice off the back foot, I was very susceptible – as indeed many batsmen are – to a very quick yorker.

It had been a wonderful series for me. At the start of it, I was an untried player with no real pedigree or long-term future – little more than a stop-gap. Yet I made good runs against high-class bowling and took a few useful wickets, most of them in the top half of the order. Strange as it may seem, I never felt ill-at-ease during that series. It was almost as if I knew the fates would look after me. After all, they hadn't done so badly before, so why should I worry over-much about fortune? I liked the fact that the West Indian bowlers attacked, so that there were plenty of runs to be picked up against positive field-settings, provided you were bold enough to have a go. Every Test after Lord's was a bonus to me. I wouldn't have complained if I'd never been picked again. But I was determined to battle and do my best whenever I played for England and I don't think I was a disaster against a great side with a wonderful inspiration in Sobers.

It had also been a good season for me at county level and I flew out to South Africa a happy, fulfilled man. I was treated like a lord out there by my own people; everyone wanted to look at my England sweater and cap. So many wanted to know what the crown and lion signified and the question and answer sessions exhausted me. I couldn't complain, though, because it was the kindness, encouragement and fund-raising ability of these people that brought me to that England cap and sweater. It was the first time I'd been back in six years and I couldn't get over the depth of interest in my exploits in the English game. The hospitality and sincere pleasure in my performances were touching and deep and I travelled 12,000 miles in two months to coach and lecture on cricket.

There was one more trip before the start of the 1967 season – to Barbados to play for the Rest of the World in a match to mark the island's independence. I was in the same side as people like Lawry, Kanhai, Graveney, McKenzie and Gibbs. Eight of the Barbados side had visited England the previous year. I suppose Barbados were a little cheeky to imagine they could take on the Rest of the World but if Gary Sobers had been fit enough, I'm sure they would have given us a hard game. It was a marvellous honour to represent such a side and my self-confidence after those early tours with Ron Roberts can well be imagined. I didn't really do much in the game, however, because Charlie Griffith hit me on the toe with a very fast delivery and I struggled for the rest of the game. But at least I could stand and watch a magnificent hundred at the other end from John Murray. He had already shown at the Oval how well he could bat and he now went out and dominated them. I could never work out why John Murray didn't make more runs.

The 1967 series against India and Pakistan were just stepping stones to a three-point plan that was beginning to formulate in my mind. Ahead was the trip to the West Indies on the following winter, then a home series against Australia and a few months later, an England tour to South Africa. I began to have visions about stepping on to Newlands as an England player – if only that could happen! I realized things might get difficult but I thought all I had to do was keep my form so that they just had to pick me for the South African tour. So I used the home Tests against India and Pakistan to consolidate my place.

I got my first Test hundred in the Leeds Test against India. No offence to the genial Indians but it was hardly memorable – because of injuries they only had three front-line bowlers and even their skipper, Pataudi, had to bowl. He later apologized to us for the fact that he had to turn his arm over. So all I did was accumulate runs and pick up my century. It's funny, though, but a lot of my best performances over the years have been at Leeds. It was the only ground in England where I seemed to get a hundred per cent support; the crowds there were always marvellous to me. If I had to play a Test innings for my life and I was allowed to pick the ground, I would plump always for Leeds with its marvellous atmosphere, excellent batting wicket and a crowd that was fiercely loyal to Yorkshire as well as English cricket.

This was the Test when Geoff Boycott batted interminably for 246 not out, and then was dropped for slow scoring. He and I were due to resume the innings on the second day when Doug Insole, the chairman of the selectors, came in and read the riot act. He said we should take account of the spectators and that the Indians had hardly any bowlers. In other words, give the crowd something to enjoy. The warning was obviously addressed to Boycott, who said nothing. Anyway, when it was time to go out to the middle, 'Boycs' led the way and our skipper, Brian Close, said to me just as I was leaving, 'Tell Boycs to take no notice, just play his natural game.' That's exactly what he did, and then he got dropped for slow scoring!

In the second innings, we had a good laugh at Boycott's expense; he was always telling us how hard it was to face the new ball, that he had the responsibility to set up a platform for the innings, etc, etc. We never had any doubts about the man's qualities, perhaps he had. Anyway, we didn't need very much to win, so the batting order was changed and 'Boycs' – who'd been going through a bit of a bad patch for Yorkshire – dropped down the order. At the end, Ray Illingworth and I put on 30-odd to win the game, with Boycott sitting in the pavilion, waiting to come in – and the lads told me he was a nervous wreck! He couldn't wait to get to the crease, something I suppose opening batsmen normally don't have to worry about. For our part, we were glad he had a taste at last of what we went through as we sat for hours with our pads on.

We won the next Test at Lord's by an innings and with their two best batsmen (Borde and Pataudi) picking up just 11 runs in four innings, that was inevitable. Tom Graveney got another hundred and the chief pleasure for many was to watch the Indian spinners wheel in, over after over. Prasanna, Chandrasekhar and Bedi were all high-class bowlers; they took 9 of England's 10 wickets in our innings and between them, they bowled 116 overs. The crowd loved it, and looking back, I wonder how good a side India would have been if those fine spinners had been backed up by a class seam bowler like Kapil Dev.

I was dropped for the Third Test at Edgbaston – 'rested' is perhaps a better word to use. The selectors wanted to take a look at Dennis Amiss to assess him with the tour of the West Indies in mind. Nothing personal against Dennis, but I felt that if a guy wants a place, then he has to earn it at the expense of someone who is below par. I felt the same way when Bob Taylor was given his maiden Test ahead of Alan Knott in New Zealand in 1971. Knotty had just finished a magnificent tour of Australia, but because Bob had been a characteristically good team-man, they decided to let him play in one Test. Knotty wasn't happy; a Test Match is a Test Match and you should pick your best available team at all times. I felt the same way in 1967 – I was averaging over 80 against the Indians, so why should I drop out?

The First Test against Pakistan that year was especially memorable to me for an example of the plusses and minusses of playing with that lovely character, Colin Milburn. Now I rated Colin very highly as an attacking batsman. He played the game the way I liked to play it and although he would often give the bowlers a chance, he could get a lot of runs on the board in no time at all. But Colin couldn't usually resist temptation and Tom Graveney went mad at him when he got himself out in this Test. Colin loved to hook and each time the ball was bounced, he'd crack it wide of the fielders. Eventually they had three men out on the leg-side boundary and he was caught trying one hook too many. Tom was the next man in and he was mad at Colin as he passed him on the way out. At the interval, he tore into Colin – 'You're too busy pleasing yourself and the crowd, what about your mates in the dressing room who're waiting to go into bat?' It's true you could get heart failure waiting to go in when Colin was at the crease – but I think he was great value and how could you change Colin Milburn?

The brightest memory for me from that rain-affected summer was Asif Iqbal's hundred at the Oval. Pakistan were down and out when he and Intikhab Alam came together – 65 for 8, to be precise. But young Asif played a beautiful innings – his footwork was masterly and he scored runs at a hell of a rate, considering the state of the game. At the other end, Intikhab – a man who subsequently proved his batting worth with Surrey – gave him great support until Asif was stumped off Close in the over before tea. We used to pull Closey's leg about being a 'Golden Arm' and, indeed, although he often conned people out, he wasn't that bad a bowler.

It wasn't a great summer for Test cricket in England but I had no complaints. I had added another five caps to my tally, I was still learning how the game should be played and I wasn't letting the side down. But the tension I would associate with Test cricket wasn't there; without being too patronizing, both India and Pakistan were going through transitional periods and they didn't have much to offer at this stage, apart from a few class batsmen, some excellent spinners, two good wicket-keepers (Engineer and Wasim Bari) and an endearingly modest and philosophical approach to Tests. I preferred the West Indian and the Australian approach – stern, unyielding defence when necessary and crushing attack at the right moment. That's how Test cricket should be played – no quarter asked or given. During that 1967 summer of Test cricket, I hardly bothered to watch a ball from the dressing-room, compared to the previous summer against the West Indians, when I was glued to every bit of it. The pattern of play was too predictable in 1967. Four years later, when the Indians and the Pakistanis shared another twin tour, things were completely different and we had some great tussles.

So my first couple of years in Test cricket were at an end. I had met some wonderful people and taken part in some great moments already. Everything seemed plain sailing with the trip to South Africa just a year away. But now things started to go wrong. The main action was beginning to move away from the cricket field.

5 West Indies 1967-8

This was the tour that gave ammunition to those who said the England selectors were right to omit me from the trip to South Africa because I couldn't cope with overseas conditions. Well, I like to think my subsequent performances in Pakistan and Australia helped to knock that theory on the head, but there was no doubt in my mind that at the time I thought the West Indian tour had spoiled things for me in my dream to play for England in South Africa.

Things went wrong right from the start. On reflection I made a grave error in going back to South Africa for a short holiday before the trip. Because I was playing my cricket in England, I wasn't prepared for the absolute barrage of advice and innuendo thrown at me when I arrived in Cape Town. I couldn't believe it – many of my friends kept saying, 'You didn't have a very good series against Pakistan, Bas. Are you worried about the South African tour?' Others would say, 'You've got to make a statement – tell the world you are available to tour South Africa with England.' Some thought I was in danger of becoming an 'Uncle Tom' by playing for white England against white South Africa; others suggested that the England selectors would gently ease me out of things over the next year, that any slight lapse of form would be crucial. Wherever I went in Cape Town, I faced the same question, 'Are you coming back with England?' I felt pulled and tugged to bits, and seemed to spend most of my time answering questions.

That short holiday was the worst thing I could have done because I was a nervous wreck by the time I met up with the England lads in London. It was by this time clear to me that most of the non-white community in South Africa so desperately wanted me to make that trip to my homeland that any deterioration in my cricket deeds would be misconstrued. They wouldn't see a lapse of form as a human failing, they would read sinister things into it, like 'perhaps Bas doesn't really want to go through with it at all'. And when I got to the

West Indies, there was no let-up in the hassle; I became aware that many black people expected me to take sides. They kept coming up to me, telling me that there was a subtler form of racial discrimination on their islands – that blacks couldn't join the golf or the yacht clubs. I sensed an underlying colour problem just bubbling to the surface in the Caribbean on that trip – and it disturbed me.

I can't totally blame non-cricketing distractions for my poor form in the West Indies. If Ray Illingworth had been skipper, I think I would have been kept in line. I realize now I accepted far too many invitations to dinner parties and receptions; at the time I was flattered that I received far more invitations than the rest of the England side put together but I got carried away by the hospitality. Wherever I went the invitations came thick and fast – and with them, came the questions about apartheid. I felt I was being asked to cure the ills of the world. Me, a simple cricketer! I thought, 'I'll have to accept all these invitations because if I don't, they'll say I'm a white Englishman and don't want to mix with the blacks, or that I'm into the Black Power Movement and don't want to be seen in white company.' In my own mind, I tried too hard to please everybody.

Some of the men associated with West Indian cricket didn't help, either. One dear old friend, a West Indian Test cricketer, worried me a little. As I was standing beside a half-caste friend of mine, who happened to look more white than coloured, he said, 'I want you to come to lunch, Bas, but don't bring that white man with you.' Clearly he hadn't forgotten the insults he'd experienced in previous years. On another occasion, a former West Indian skipper, who was a white man, invited the England side on to his boat. Some of the West Indian players heard about this and they told me, 'You won't see any black men on that boat, not even us. We won't be invited.' They were right.

I wasn't allowed to get the racial thing out of my mind, even if I had been strong-willed enough to try to fight it. Every time I went out to bat in the series, I kept thinking to myself, 'I've got to get runs because some people will think I'm not trying, that I want to stay out of trouble and miss out on the South African trip.' All this at a time when I was struggling to find my touch anyway. I didn't start the tour all that well and I ran out of games in which to find true form. Edrich, Boycott, Graveney, Cowdrey and Barrington all played well and I never seemed to get in for very long. As a batsman, I always reacted best to pressure and I didn't face all that much of it on the field because our early batsmen were so prolifically successful. But I must be honest – batting is very much a mental thing and on that tour, I was never right in that department.

Colin Cowdrey had been appointed captain in place of Brian Close after a fairly sensational sequence of events at the end of the 1967 summer. Close had been censured for time-wasting tactics on the field with Yorkshire and he had allegedly assaulted a spectator at Edgbaston. I think Brian Close was sold short over this – I believe the Establishment were looking for an excuse to bounce him out of a tour that they knew would pose many problems of diplomacy. It would be a difficult tour but I reckon Closey would have been sensible enough to behave the right way. I think he got saddled with a reckless image from his youth that he never threw off and which obscured his great gifts as an attacking captain. The fact that he has been an England selector in recent years may have helped to soften the blow about being passed over after winning six Tests out of seven as captain – but I'm not so sure. Close was too rational and proud of playing for England to be tempted to live up to his firebrand image; in his time as England captain, I never had any complaints about the way he treated me. The same can be said about Colin Cowdrey, a decent, fair-minded man whom I became very close to during the traumatic events later in 1968. Colin did a fine job on that West Indies tour and the team spirit was excellent under his leadership but it's ironic that he won the series using the same kind of blatant go-slow tactics that got Brian Close into hot water the previous summer.

The First Test at Port of Spain gave us hope that perhaps this great West Indian side was beginning to get a little frayed round the edges. We'd always thought they relied too much on the great Gary Sobers and the series proved us right. Anyway we rattled up a big total with Tom Graveney playing one of his most beautiful knocks for England and although the gangling Clive Lloyd hit a century in his first Test, the West

Indies had to follow on. The game was heading for a draw just before tea on the final day when my room-mate, David Brown, took three wickets in an over – Butcher, Murray and Griffith. What a great whole-hearted player 'Hovis' Brown was! If there was half-an-hour to go before close of play, and one batsman had a hundred to his name and the other was in the fifties and the bowlers were scared stiff of catching the captain's eye, it was always Brown who'd volunteer to bowl. No day was too long for him, no cause too hopeless and it was typical of him that he'd break through on such a dead wicket. Anyway, with just two wickets to fall, we thought we were in with a great chance of snatching a victory. Wes Hall came in to partner Gary Sobers and Brown's first ball after tea popped off Wes Hall's bat and just went over Boycott's head at short leg. We would have won that game if that catch had gone in, because there was only Lance Gibbs to come and even Sobers couldn't bat at both ends! In the end, Wes and Gary batted very well and played out time.

The next Test was one of the most dramatic I can recall – and mostly for the wrong reasons. It started off badly for me, when I was the victim of a terrible umpiring decision. I never moved my foot to David Holford's leg-spinner and Derryck Murray took the bails off out of habit. But he appealed and I was thunderstruck when I was given out. Many of the West Indian players told me afterwards I was never out of my crease but that was no consolation. I know luck evens itself out over a career and that I've been more fortunate than most, but I was beginning to think that my luck was ebbing away fast on that tour just when I needed it most.

By the time the West Indies batted, the Kingston wicket was cracking up. John Snow – brought into the team because we thought the wicket would suit him – took seven wickets and he, Brown and Jeff Jones bowled magnificently in searing heat. They gave everything they had and at close of play, they could hardly speak or stand up, and they went straight to bed to prepare for the attempted breakthrough in the West Indians' second knock after we'd asked them to follow on. I was particularly impressed by the efforts of John Snow. It seemed he often only bowled when he felt like it but there was no faulting his attitude or his commitment on that day. When Snowy saw bounce or movement for him in a wicket, he was a different bowler and he was to prove a godsend to us in this series.

So they followed on, more than 200 behind, and we started to whittle away at them. We had four down and they were still more than 60 behind when Gary Sobers came in. By this time, the gaps in the wicket were about 2 inches wide and it was simply a case of getting Sobers out to win the match. Early on he nicked one along the ground through the slips and Tom Graveney hurt a nail trying to stop the ball. He went off for running repairs and Colin Cowdrey called me from mid-off to stand in the slips while Tom was being sorted out. I was worried stiff because my catching was getting to be as bad as my form with the bat and I had an uneasy feeling about what was going to happen. It did. After my protests had been ignored by Colin, the very next ball by Brown was snicked by Gary to me at slip. I dropped a straightforward catch, and in the process saved the Test for the West Indies. At the end of the over, Tom returned to the field. I had stood for just three balls at slip and, in the process, mucked things up.

There was more drama to come, though. Basil Butcher played me down the leg-side and Jim Parks took a good catch behind the stumps. No doubt at all about the validity of the catch and Butcher walked straight away. Then all hell was let loose. The crowd rioted – all sorts of things were thrown on to the field. Clearly the crowd didn't savour the prospect of an England win and also the daily intake of rum was beginning to take its toll. Anyway, after Colin and Gary had failed to appease the crowd, the riot police were called in. We started walking towards the pavilion and they turned on the tear gas to disperse the crowd. But nobody had told these guys that there was a slight wind about, so by the time we'd got to the pavilion, we could hardly see. The gas was in our eyes, ears and noses and it was the most sickening feeling. By this time the English dressing-room contained every frightened Englishman on the ground, including the press. Someone said, 'Put your heads under water to get rid of the gas' and there we all were, soaked to the skin under the showers trying to see!

Calm of an uneasy sort descended on the Kingston ground and after about an hour and a half's delay, there was an announcement that play would resume. Most of the spectators had vanished and there was an eerie feeling as I prepared to continue my over. Some ring-leader must have been watching all this because just as I started to run up to bowl, over the top they came. They hurled bottles, fruit, stones, everything you could think of, and we had to call off play for the day.

That effectively ruined our chance of winning the match, and indeed we nearly lost it. The next day Gary Sobers celebrated his reprieve at my hands to play a most remarkable innings. By this time the wicket was like the face of the moon – the cracks were getting wider and wider and if the ball pitched on one side of the crack, it would shoot along the deck and if it pitched elsewhere, it would take off. Against two bowlers like Snow and Brown, batting was a hazardous business but Gary played a masterpiece of an innings, sheer genius in fact. Anybody who scored 20 on that wicket had done well.

Gary realized that batting was now a complete lottery so he declared and set us a target of 158 to win. We had little hope of getting that unless someone played a great innings and soon we were 0 for 2 with Cowdrey and Boycott out to Sobers himself. At the end of the fifth day, we were told that we had to play another ninety minutes the following day to make up for the time lost through the riots. Charming, we thought, we could lose this Test because of the riots that we hadn't caused.

I was next man in and my thoughts as Jim Parks was nearly decapitated by a nasty lifter can well be imagined. The ground was packed (no admission charges) and when Jim was out early, I went in to join Tom Graveney, who was battling away and making things look comparatively easy. By this time, Tom was in a fair old temper and feeling a little bloody-minded about the whole business. At 11.40, after forty minutes' play, we were entitled to call for drinks and I said to Tom, 'What shall we do?' 'We're having those drinks,' he said. The crowd weren't happy about that and these two little guys came tearing on to the field with the drinks trolley. I've never seen drinks handed out so quickly! There were about another forty minutes to go before the game was due to finish, we had five wickets left, the West Indian players hadn't moved from their positions, Gary Sobers was standing at his bowling mark with the ball in his hand – but Tom and I were standing in the middle of the wicket sipping our drinks. 'It's a lonely feeling, this is, Tom', I said, and then he had a go at the drinks blokes. 'On Saturday, when we were winning the game you strolled out but today, you run out with the drinks,' he told them. That did it – one of the West Indians overheard this and walked over to Tom – 'Leave them out of it, it's nothing to do with them, take it out on us.' Tom replied, 'I don't give a damn, I just feel that way. As a matter of fact, I bloody well feel like going home!'

Tom's mood wasn't improved when he was dismissed in curious circumstances. He lapped an off-break to Lance Gibbs but unfortunately it hit short leg on the hip and then it lobbed over to Charlie Griffith at wide mid-on, the only fielder not near the bat. Tom was annoyed and the next day when he read a newspaper report, he got even more angry – the report said his dismissal was due to 'another irresponsible shot from Graveney'.

I was then joined by Fred Titmus and we were doing our best to occupy that last half-hour with anything other than actually facing many deliveries on that unbelievable wicket. The West Indians were rushing around trying to get their overs in but we didn't think that one of their umpires would help them keep the tempo flowing! It happened when Douglas Sang Hue moved from square leg to square on the off-side because too many fielders were crowding round the bat. Titmus pushed forward to a delivery and just nudged it out on the off-side, only for Sang Hue to pick up the ball and throw it back to the bowler! Fred asked pointedly, 'Whose side are you on, umpire?' That slow-moving ball out of reach of the fielders meant valuable time to us, yet there was the umpire picking up the ball to keep things moving!

There was one more astonishing moment to come. Fred got out right at the end and David Brown came in to face what proved to be the final over. Sobers was bowling off six paces and he bowled the most vicious bouncer I've ever seen. David was pushing forward and I don't know how it missed him – it just took off vertically and parted his hair. David still talks about it to this day! Anyway, Sobers bowled him off the last ball, to leave them two wickets short of victory. I was sure there was time for another over but I thought, 'I'll try to bluff them', and I walked off with David. To my surprise, they all followed me without a peep.

I was shattered at the end of what was a remarkable Test. Six days of tension, interspersed with a riot, some odd umpiring decisions and a wicket that was very, very dangerous to bat on. Somehow we had held on when everything was against us and we were beginning to feel that although the West Indies had more talent, we were a more integrated, professional side and that our chance would come again.

There was no elbow room for a victory push in the next Test at Bridgetown. On a superb batting strip, there were just too many runs about and we simply concentrated on 'what we have, we hold'. We were jockeying for an opening and it came in the next Test at Port of Spain.

We got a great press for scoring at a rate of 78 an hour to reach a victory target of 215 with just three wickets down but in truth, it was our defensive tactics on the field that frustrated Gary Sobers into making a declaration. On the last morning, with nothing left in the game, we were bowling only 11 six-ball overs an hour, which I thought was pretty disgraceful. Colin was hanging on to what we had and he was determined that they wouldn't take control of the game. In the end Gary just got fed up and he called his batsmen in to see if England would make a game of it when it was our turn to bat. It was a brave declaration, really, because Charlie Griffith was injured and he only had three front-line bowlers, but I think he felt a protest was more important than just letting the game die on its feet.

We started well on the run-chase and at tea, we needed about another 140 in 90 minutes – but still Colin had to be persuaded to go for the runs, even though we had nine wickets in hand. In the dressing-room there was a big discussion between Edrich, Graveney and Cowdrey and I got the impression that John and Tom were trying to force Colin to chase victory. Before play re-started, Colin came over to me and said, 'If we lose a wicket quickly, Tom will come in. If Geoff Boycott and I go on well for a while, I want you in next.' Well, Colin went out there and played magnificently; he caressed the ball around as if he was batting against boys. In the end I joined Geoff Boycott and hit the winning run with a couple of overs to spare. At no stage did Gary Sobers try to close up the game by slowing down the over-rate.

Gary took some terrible stick for his declaration but to be fair to him, not many sides score 78 an hour on the last day of a Test. It just wasn't Gary's style to play defensively for very long and he had no time for the argument that you could kill a game stone dead to avoid giving the opposition the chance to win a Test. I've talked to him subsequently about that declaration and he told me that he would do the same again because he was so disgusted at our tactics in the field on that final morning. But he took the defeat well, he was that kind of cricketer.

It was a lucky win for us – but we'd taken our chance. So now we had to hold firm in the final Test to win a series against all odds. We managed it – but only just. Kanhai and Sobers had one of their rare big partnerships together – a little matter of 250 – and they absolutely murdered us. They tried to outscore each other and the only beneficiaries of that rivalry were the spectators. Gary made 152 and 95 not out in that game, and he took six wickets – yet some sections of the crowd still booed him for his declaration in the previous Test. In the end we hung on for the draw with poor Jeff Jones having to play out an entire over from Lance Gibbs. Considering that Jeff averaged two with the bat in this series, that wasn't a bad performance from our Welsh friend! None of us could watch in the dressing-room with our last pair together. How Jeff got through those six balls I will never know.

It was sweet to win the series after so many people had written us off at the start. We knew Sobers would be the big danger, because he could win a match on his own and that would have meant we had to snatch victories in two Tests. Cowdrey's method of holding things together on the good wickets and waiting for the opportunity to strike paid off handsomely. It was a defensive strategy, I agree, but if we had gone all out to attack the West Indians, they would have murdered us. Brian Close would have attacked more, but I don't think his tactics would have brought more success than Colin's cat-and-mouse strategy.

John Snow bowled magnificently. He chose the right line

– just outside the off stump – because he realized that if you bowled at the stumps, their batsmen would just smash the ball through mid-wicket or past mid-on. Brown and Jones gave tremendous support, Alan Knott blossomed into a fine wicket-keeper/batsman and all our top batsmen did well, apart from B. L. D'Oliveira. Socially it was a great tour for me but my cricketing was disappointing. I just never got going – I batted at number seven, behind Jim Parks, in three of the Tests – and there were few occasions when the chips were really down when I came to the wicket. One of them was at Kingston in the Second Test and I don't think I failed then. I was wrong to try to please everybody when the invitations kept flooding in – I was too keen to create a good impression. All I got in return was more pressure, as the conflicting opinions about my possible selection to tour South Africa rained down on my head.

I'm sure some of my team-mates were annoyed at the way I reacted to the tour – and looking back, I agree with them. But nobody said anything to me, not even Colin Cowdrey, my captain. I must clear up one point, though. When I wasn't picked initially for the South African tour, it was suggested in the press that perhaps I wasn't a good tourist, that my good conduct money had been withheld after the tour to the West Indies. Totally untrue – I was paid the £150 bonus in full.

As we flew back at the start of April, I was conscious that momentous things were happening. I hoped for the best, I dearly wanted to make that trip to South Africa in six months' time – but I knew that the events of the last few months hadn't exactly consolidated my position in the minds of the selectors.

6 The D'Oliveira Affair 1968

I'll never forget the events of summer 1968 as long as I live. It was a nightmare, punctuated by occasional bouts of euphoria. Actions that had little to do with events on the cricket field meant that South Africa would inevitably be barred from Test cricket and, indeed, from most international sport. And the unwitting reason for that ban? Me. Even now, after all these years, I still have difficulty sorting out fact from fiction, half-truth from allegation. The rumour machine certainly worked overtime during that period, with my name stuck right in the middle. Before examining things in any great detail, just consider these facts and consider the ironies contained therein.

1   January 1967 – Britain's Sports Minister, Denis Howell, told a cheering House of Commons that the 1968/9 tour to South Africa would be cancelled if there were any moves to ban me.

2   In the same month, South Africa's Minister of the Interior, Mr Piet Le Roux said, 'We will not allow mixed teams to play against our white teams over here. If this player is chosen, he would not be allowed to come here. Our policy is well known here and overseas.'

3   April 1967 – South Africa's Prime Minister, Mr John Vorster, said that apartheid principles would be relaxed in so far as they affected teams from overseas countries 'with whom we have traditional sporting ties'.

4   September 1967 – Derek Dowling, a South African Test selector, told me he was sure I'd be allowed to go on tour, if selected.

5   March 1968 – Sir Alec Douglas-Home met Mr Vorster in South Africa and came to the conclusion that my chances of being allowed to tour South Africa were favourable.

6   A few weeks later, Lord Cobham, a former President of the MCC, was asked to visit Mr Vorster while in South

Africa. He later said, 'Mr Vorster gave me to suppose that if D'Oliveira were selected, the tour would probably have to be cancelled.' Lord Cobham passed his opinion on to the appropriate MCC officials.

7   June 1968 – Wilfred Isaacs, a prominent man in South African cricket, came to see me at Lord's and talked warmly about the forthcoming tour. He offered me his flat and hospitality whenever I wanted it on the trip. Yet when he returned to South Africa a few weeks later, he forecast to the press that I would not be selected. He also later denied he'd spoken about the tour to any MCC officials.

8   June 1968 – A high-ranking official told me on the eve of the Lord's Test that I could get everyone out of trouble by making myself available for South Africa, *not* England. I angrily refused.

9   August 1968 – Tiene Oosthuizen, an official working for a tobacco company, offered me a £40,000 ten-year contract, plus a car and a house, to coach in South Africa . . . provided I announced I was unavailable for the South African tour *before* the Fifth Test. I declined his offer.

10   August 1968 – I was left out of the tour party. The MCC Secretary, Mr S. C. Griffith, said, 'Nothing else was discussed at the selectors' meeting other than cricketing considerations.' With scores that included 158 and 87 not out in the series, I was top of the England batting averages and second in the bowling averages.

11   It was revealed that two of the eight men who picked the tour party knew of Lord Cobham's warning that the tour would probably be cancelled if I was picked. But apparently, for reasons best known to themselves, they didn't tell the other six selectors what they knew. However, Doug Insole, the chairman of the selectors, said, 'All I can say is that I was not aware any selectors knew about Lord Cobham's report.'

12   September 1968 – Tom Cartwright broke down through injury and I was summoned to take his place in the tour party; a batsman replacing a bowler.

13   September 1968 – Mr Vorster denounced my selection
and said, 'It is the team of the anti-apartheid movement'.
The MCC called off the tour because the reconstituted
party was unacceptable to Mr Vorster and his Government.

When the tour was cancelled I felt terribly sad for the
players, for people like Colin Milburn and Pat Pocock, who'd
also been left out; nobody had taken up cudgels on their
behalf, it was all about D'Oliveira. I kept thinking, 'Their
Government can't refuse South Africa just for me, can they?'
and I then realized, 'This thing must be very big to Vorster'. I
realized the political aspect of it all was even greater than I had
imagined. I understand Vorster was facing a revolt within his
Nationalist Party from the right-wing, anti-liberal element and
he clearly felt he had to clamp down to assert his authority.
The game of cricket gave him that opportunity.
    Right from the day I'd been selected to play for England
in 1966, this trip had been on my mind. I knew what was
needed from me on the tour – I'd act like a sportsman all the
way through, I'd leave all the media interviews to the captain
and the manager. I desperately wanted to show the world that
there was nothing wrong with the non-whites in South Africa,
that we *could* conduct ourselves in the proper manner, that
there would be no trouble if blacks played whites on the sports
field. But from the day I first played for England, I'd been
pulled this way and that by various people, all with definite
views on colour and its significance to my case. I'd get letters
by the hundred, the phone at home and in the Worcester
dressing-room would be ringing all the time with advice at
hand for me. I was just a simple cricketer, conscious of the
debt I owed to both the white man in England and to my own
people in Cape Town. I lacked the intellectual capacity to
think it through in those days so I tried to use my cricketing
skills to make statements on behalf of the non-white community.
    All I knew was that if I played well enough in the 1968
season, then I surely had a chance of being selected. Oh, I'd
read about all sorts of rumours in the press about the attitudes
of various politicians but I thought, 'I'll let them sort it all out

later, for the time being I've got to prove myself all over again.' As soon as I got back home from the West Indies, I was getting messages from South Africa which said, in effect, 'We told you so, you're not trying on the field anymore, because you've been got at. You don't want to come back here as a player because you don't want to spoil things for the white man.' I tried to tell them that I just didn't play very well out in the West Indies, but it was hopeless.

I worked out a strategy – and I have to admit, it involved playing for myself and thinking selfishly about my cricket, something I hope I haven't done too much in my career. For this short period, considerations of my team-mates went out of the window because that trip to South Africa was the most important thing in my life at that time. I realized that I would have a good chance of playing in the First Test, purely because we'd won the series in the West Indies and because all things being equal, the selectors usually keep faith with a successful side for at least one Test at home. So if I was picked at the start, I had to make that one match count and consolidate my position in the team. The next Test would be at Lord's, so that if I did well first time round, I was bound to get another chance at Leeds, Edgbaston and the Oval which were batsmens' paradises. All I needed was a good start to show that my bad patch in the West Indies was behind me.

I confided my plan to Naomi, nobody else. She said, 'Just try your best, Bas, I know what it means to you.' In those early weeks of the 1968 season, the press was playing down the whole thing in case the selectors thought they were being pressurized. All the time the pressures from the black community were getting unbearable. Friends of mine from Cape Town would visit me at the Worcester ground and tell me that the talk back home was that I wasn't bothered about the tour. No matter how long I talked about it to them, it never made any impact. I would just have to prove them wrong on the cricket field, if I could only get the chance. I heard about the visits of Lord Cobham and Sir Alec Douglas-Home and the conflicting opinions they had brought back, but as far as I was concerned, it was just talk. I had to do my stuff on the cricket field, to *make* the selectors pick me – and leave the political side to the politicians.

When I heard I'd been picked for the First Test of the season, it felt like Beaconsfield 1966 all over again. 'Now's your chance, Bas,' I told myself, 'if you muck this one up, you're finished. Don't give anyone any more excuses to drop you.' As far as I'm concerned, I played very well at Old Trafford. The wicket was tricky all the way through and in the last innings, with the ball turning so much that even Bob Cowper was made to look a good off-spinner, I made 87 not out. I remember Graham McKenzie giving me a hell of a time for about 20 minutes, bowling round the wicket. The angle was totally different, the ball kept rearing up off a length and I really gritted my teeth and talked myself through it – 'Come on, Bas, you can be a star of this game if you see him off. You blew it in the West Indies but all you need to do is get some runs here and they've just got to pick you from now on.' Well, I stayed in, and although we lost the match, I felt I had re-established myself in the England side.

So much for taking things for granted. Because we lost that Test, the selectors had to think about re-shaping a side that had gone into the Manchester match with a very unbalanced bowling attack. I was the third seamer which was surely wrong; I should always be a batsman who could be the sixth bowler as a bonus. John Snow and David Brown needed a back-up seamer but I didn't think I would be the one to be sacrificed. I was already planning my strategy, hoping that we would either lose the toss and have to field or we would bat so well that I wouldn't have to bat on the first day. I believed that the Lord's wicket is always at its liveliest on the first day and that afterwards, the batsman has a good chance of making runs.

On the morning of the match. I was in the nets when Colin Cowdrey came to me and said, 'Bas, I'm sorry but I have to make you twelfth man. We need Barry Knight as the extra seamer. I know you did very well up at Old Trafford and that you're disappointed, but before the season is out, you'll be back.' I went into the dressing-room, put on my blazer and asked if there were any tickets to be taken to the gate (that's one of the twelfth man duties at a Test). Nobody said a word in the dressing-room, it had obviously come as a surprise to some of the lads. As I walked out to the gate, peo-

ple were milling round me, shouting, 'Best of luck today, Bas'
and all those other heart-warming greetings I had always
treasured; but my heart was heavy. I was pondering the significance of missing this Test. I had done my stuff at Manchester, yet now I was out. What would happen if the lads played
well here? The selectors wouldn't change a winning side.

In my mind I turned over a curious incident from the
previous evening. At the pre-Test dinner, a top cricket official told me that the only way the tour could be saved
would be if I announced I was unavailable for *England* but
would like to play for *South Africa*. I was staggered and angrily
said, 'Either you respect me as an England player or you
don't.' The next day, an eminent cricket writer put the same
proposition to me. Things were getting out of hand, I
thought. Then came the visit to the England dressing-room
from Wilfred Isaacs. Doug Insole brought him in to see me
and as usual, he greeted me warmly and talked enthusiastically
about the part I would be playing on the tour. I said I'd be
happy to accept his offer of hospitality if I went on tour; after
all, he was known as a very generous host and a real cricket
benefactor in the Republic. I don't know how close he was to
the politicians but he was very much a 'backroom boy' in
South African cricket.

A couple of weeks after our amicable conversation in the
Lord's dressing-room, Mr Isaacs told the South African press
that I would *not* be selected; he also denied that he'd spoken
about my selection to MCC officials. So how did he know I
wouldn't be picked? It was all getting rather curious.

England played splendidly in that Second Test and only
the rain saved Australia from a crushing defeat. The policy of
selecting three seamers was triumphantly vindicated. I gave up
thinking about England because I thought there was no hope
now of me getting back in. The next three Tests were all on
batsmens' wickets and it would take a lot to dislodge the present team, especially if they turned their undoubted edge over a
mediocre Australian side into tangible victories. I lost all
interest in cricket for a while, I didn't socialise back in Worcester and I moped around. I was hurt about being dropped after
doing so well at Old Trafford and my form started to slip
away. I knew that only a series of injuries would get me back

in contention. I trusted Colin Cowdrey as a gentleman and his words kept coming back to me that I would be back soon, but deep down I was conscious that there was now something bigger at stake than just the wishes of an ordinary professional cricketer. However much I trusted that I would get a square deal in England, I knew other factors occasionally determined that certain individuals become irrelevant and unimportant.

Enter Tiene Oosthuizen, the next member of the increasingly odd circle I was finding myself in. At that time he was the UK managing director of the Carreras Tobacco Company of which Rothmans is a subsidiary. Mr Oosthuizen asked me to come and see him in London as soon as possible to discuss a business venture. I agreed and found myself being offered £4,000 a year for the next ten years with a car, house and generous expenses thrown in for good measure. All I had to do was leave for South Africa as soon as the English season had ended to take up the job of cricket coach and sports organizer for an organization called the South African Foundation. He said he wanted a man to look after facilities for coloured South Africans. The offer, of course, was very tempting but there were two snags: I had to declare myself unavailable for the England tour *and* make my announcement before August 14th. The MCC tour party was due to be announced on August 28th and Mr Oosthuizen said he had to let the Sports Foundation know my answer within a fortnight. I was suspicious about the need for haste and his assurances that the offer had nothing to do with politics. I knew I could not accept while there was still an outside chance of realizing my lifetime's ambition. It would insult my own people, the ones who were as desperate for me to get on that trip as I was.

I told him I wouldn't prejudice my chances of being selected for the tour and he replied, 'If you knew you would *not* be accepted in South Africa as a member of that tour, would you then take the job?' I pointed out that nobody could know whether I would be accepted. He replied, 'Well, I can.' He said he had enough contacts in political circles to get an answer within a few days. I said, 'Find out for me and we'll talk again.' We met at the Excelsior Motel near Oxford on the following Sunday and he told me that he had it from the highest possible source that, if I was being included in the MCC side, I would be an embarrassment to the Government and to Mr Vorster. He asked me if, reading between the lines, I realized what that would mean; it would be better for me not to go. I told him I could not let so many people down by withdrawing my availability, nor would I want to. He asked me to contact him within a few days, even though I re-iterated that I would not change my mind. The whole thing was far too fishy. I was determined to keep open the door to a recall by England, even though it meant throwing away security for my wife and family. Mr Oosthuizen phoned me again before he flew out to South Africa and I found myself bluffing. I told him I'd been offered £2,000 by an organization just to stay available for the tour. 'Basil, I'll do even better if you take this job for me,' he said. My bluff had revealed how keen he was to land my services and keep me away from consideration for the tour. I stalled for time and he said he'd ring me again in a few days.

That same Sunday, the England team was announced for the final Test at the Oval – and I wasn't in it. Surely I had no chance of getting on the trip now? Was it right to deny Naomi and my two sons the chance of a superb lifestyle? My mind was in the same state it had been in all summer – one of complete turmoil.

Mr Oosthuizen rang again on the Tuesday and I made it clear that I would still like to wait until the tour party was selected in eight days' time. If I wasn't in the party, then I would be happy to take up the offer. I told him there was still an outside chance of my selection and I wanted to hang on. I stalled again and he agreed to ring me the following morning at home. He was being very persistent, affirming time after time that it was the best possible course of action for me.

I'd taken that Tuesday call in the office of Reg Hayter, my agent, and we agreed that I would try to keep the offer open for a few more days, until I knew my fate when the tour party was announced. I left London and drove slowly back to Worcester, trying to work out this fellow Oosthuizen. As my car stopped at some traffic lights in Worcester I spotted the unmistakable figure of Freddie Trueman. He greeted me with his usual banter – 'What the hell are you doing here, Bas?' That floored me for a start, because Worcester were due to play a home match against Yorkshire, starting the following day. 'You should be at the Oval with the England team,' he said. 'Roger Prideaux has pulled out and you've been named. You should be at the Oval, old son.' I thought Fred had gone off his rocker. I told him I hadn't had the car radio on while driving up from London, so he was in the clear if he wanted to continue the joke. 'Okay, come into this pub and we'll check it out with the landlord,' said Fred. 'Then you might believe me.' Inside they confirmed the news – it had just been on the radio.

I dashed back home in high excitement. At last, one more chance! On the Oval wicket against an ordinary Aussie bowling side! How could I fail? These thoughts swirled round in my mind as I hastily packed my gear. I kept wondering how the folks on Signal Hill would be reacting to my recall – and how Tiene Oosthuizen would now view the situation. The following morning, I waited for the call from Mr Oosthuizen. Dead on the appointed time, the international operator called and said, 'The call booked to you from South Africa has been cancelled. The caller is not able to talk to you.'

I never heard from, nor set eyes on Tiene Oosthuizen again. Nor did I ever find out if someone was putting up all that money to keep me away from consideration for the tour.

Coaching in South Africa would have to wait for another year. As far as I was concerned I was going on the England tour, because I just *knew* I would do well in the Oval Test. I felt as if a huge weight had been lifted from my shoulders; all I had to do was prove my ability on the cricket field. I could have hugged Roger Prideaux for dropping out with pleurisy, although Colin Milburn wasn't too happy. On the day before the Test started I joined the rest of the England team and Colin was getting worried that he too now had to prove himself to the tour selectors. After a fine start for England, in which Roger Prideaux had made an impressive half-century as an opener in a rain-affected game at Leeds, he was now out of the Oval match with suspected pleurisy, but Colin gloomily told me that Roger Prideaux looked as fit as anybody on the ground when he turned up on Wednesday. That, however, was not my problem, but Colin's. He would have to sort out his own problems for the time being because I didn't think I could possibly fail. The weather was set fair, the wicket was a flat, Oval beauty and I even had my lucky umpire, Charlie Elliott, standing in the match. Whenever Charlie stood in my games, I always seemed to do well.

Thursday dawned hot and beautiful. We batted all day and I went in with half-an-hour to go. The Aussies threw everything at me but the terrific ovation I got as I walked out to bat was enough to stiffen my resolve, if I'd needed any further incentive. The public, as usual, was behind me and I knew I wouldn't let them down the next day. I took off my pads in the dressing room and said to myself, 'Basil, you've got just one day, just one day to do it.' I didn't have a drink that night, I went back to the hotel early and slept like a log. I felt so cool and calm, as if I had a date with a century. The next morning, with the sun streaming through the window, I rang Naomi and told her I felt wonderful and she said, 'Oh Bas, I didn't sleep a wink all night.' I told her there was nothing to worry about – 'pull up a chair, turn on the TV and enjoy it, Naomi, because I'm going to be there all day.'

As I walked through the Oval gates, everybody kept wishing me good luck and I felt like a million dollars. At nets, John Edrich said, 'This is a lovely flat wicket. You could get a hundred here today.' Early on that day, I played a couple of bad shots and when I got to Charlie Elliott's end, he whispered, 'get your head down'. I kept on playing in my usual style and when I reached my fifty, Charlie whispered out of the corner of his mouth, 'Well played – my God, you're going to cause some problems.' I laughed and wondered what he'd say when I got my hundred; that's how certain I was that this was to be my day. When I lapped Johnny Gleeson for a single to reach my century, the next comment from Charlie was 'Oh Christ, the cat's among the pigeons now' and Gleeson put it a little more circumspectly – 'Well done, Bas, it'll be interesting to see what happens now.' I didn't really consider anything like that in the greatest moment of my cricketing life; I'd proved I could still play the game and now surely *nothing* could keep me out of that tour party. I just went on playing shots after that; I tried to get out but rode my luck to get 158. As far as I was concerned, those extra 58 runs weren't important. I'd got my century.

20 and **21** The scorecard and the England team for one of the most fateful Tests in cricket history – the Oval, 1968.

Surrey County Cricket Club   6d.

ENGLAND v. AUSTRALIA
at Kennington Oval, Thurs., Fri., Sat., Mon., Tues., Aug. 22nd, 23rd, 24th, 26th, 27th, 1968.

	ENGLAND		First Innings		Second Innings	
1	J. H. Edrich	Surrey	b Chappell	164	c Lawry, b Mallett	17
2	C. Milburn	Northamptonshire	b Connolly	8	c Lawry, b Connolly	18
4	E. R. Dexter	Sussex	b Gleeson	21	b Connolly	28
*3	M. C. Cowdrey	Kent	lbw b Mallett	16	b Mallett	35
5	T. W. Graveney	Worcestershire	c Redpath, b McKenzie	63	run out	12
6	B. L. D'Oliveira	Worcestershire	c Inverarity, b Mallett	158	c Gleeson, b Connolly	9
‡7	A. P. E. Knott	Kent	c Jarman, b Mallett	28	run out	34
8	R. Illingworth	Yorkshire	lbw b Connolly	8	b Gleeson	10
9	J. A. Snow	Sussex	run out	4	c Sheahan, b Gleeson	13
10	D. L. Underwood	Kent	not out	9	not out	1
11	D. J. Brown	Warwickshire	c Sheahan, b Gleeson	2	b Connolly	1
			B1 , l-b11, w1 , n-b	13	B , l-b3 , w , n-b	3

Substitute Fielder—C. T. Radley Middx

| | | Total | 494 | Total | 181 |

Fall of the wickets   1—28   2—84   3—113   4—238   5—359   6—421   7—458   8—468   9—489   10—494
                       1—23   2—53   3—67   4—90   5—114   6—126   7—149   8—179   9—179   10—181

Bowling Analysis 1st Ins.	O.	M.	R.	W.	Wd.	N.b.	2nd Ins.	O.	M.	R.	W.	Wd.	N.b.
McKenzie	40	8	87	1				4	0	14	0		
Connolly	57	12	127	2				22.4	2	65	4		
Walters	6	2	17	0	1								
Gleeson	41.2	8	109	2				7	2	22	2		
Mallett	36	11	87	3				25	4	77	2		
Chappell	21	5	54	1									

	AUSTRALIA		First Innings		Second Innings	
*1	W. M. Lawry	Victoria	c Knott, b Snow	135	c Milburn, b Brown	4
2	R. J. Inverarity	Western Australia	c Milburn, b Snow	· 1	lbw b Underwood	56
3	I. R. Redpath	Victoria	c Cowdrey, b Snow	67	lbw b Underwood	8
5	I. M. Chappell	South Australia	c Knott, b Snow	10	lbw b Underwood	2
4	K. D. Walters	New South Wales	c Knott, b Brown	5	c Knott, b Underwood	4
6	A. P. Sheahan	Victoria	b Illingworth	14	c Snow, b Illingworth	24
‡7	B. N. Jarman	South Australia	st Knott, b Illingworth	0	b D'Oliveira	21
9	G. D. McKenzie	Western Australia	b Brown	12	c Brown, b Underwood	0
8	A. Mallett	South Australia	not out	43	c Brown, b Underwood	0
10	J. W. Gleeson	New South Wales	c Dexter, b Underwood	19	b Underwood	5
11	A. N. Connolly	Victoria	b Underwood	3	not out	0
			B4 , l-b 7, w , n-b4	15	B , l-b4 , w , n-b	4

Substitute Fielder—N. J. N. Hawke

| | | Total | 324 | Total | 125 |

Fall of the wickets   1—7   2—136   3—151   4—161   5—185   6—188   7—237   8—269   9—302   10—324
                       1—4   2—13   3 19   4—29   5—65   6—110   7—110   8—110   9—120   10—125

Bowling Analysis 1st Ins.	O.	M.	R.	W.	Wd.	N.b.	2nd Ins.	O.	M.	R.	W.	Wd.	N.b.
Snow	35	12	67	3		3		11	5	22	0		
Brown	22	5	63	3				8	3	19	1		
Illingworth	48	15	87	2		1		28	18	29	1		
Underwood	54.3	21	89	2				31.3	19	50	7		
D'Oliveira	4	2	3	0				5	4	1	1		

*Captain   ‡Wkt.-keeper   Toss won by—ENGLAND

Umpires—C. S. Elliott & A. E. Fagg   Result—ENGLAND won by 226 runs

Hours of play—1st, 2nd, 3rd & 4th days 11.30—6.30.   5th day 11.0—5.30 or 6.0   Lunch 1.30 all days
NEW BALL may be taken by the fielding captain after 85 overs

£50 TOWARDS YOUR HOLIDAY.   Enquire at Supporters' Association Office.

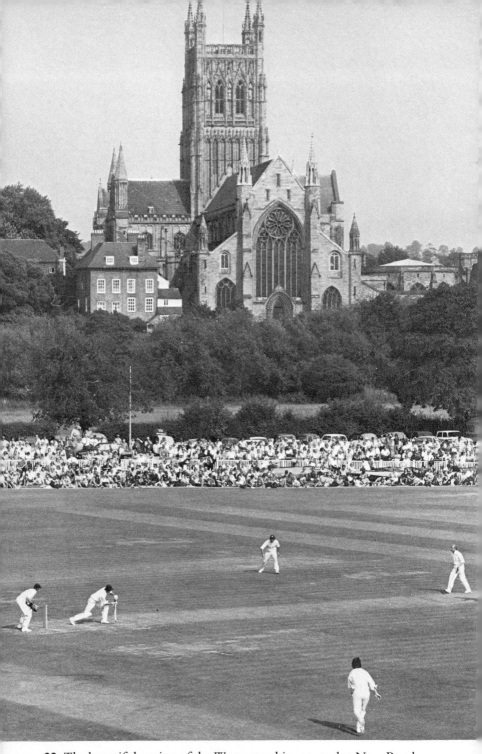

22 The beautiful setting of the Worcestershire ground at New Road.
Who wouldn't want to play cricket here?

23 and **24** Two unoriginal ways to celebrate a championship victory – but for all that, very satisfying. I'm on the far right as we toast our 1965 success, and my skipper, Norman Gifford and I celebrate the 1974 championship win in style.

25 Examining the medal and the cheque that goes with a 'Man of the Match' award – this one was at Hove in the Gillette Cup, 1974.

26 Putting a bit of beef into a Sunday League knock in 1976.

27 How did I ever manage to con so many batsmen out? Umpire David Constant probably wonders the same thing . . .

When I walked back after being dismissed, the crowd's reception was overwhelming, on a par with that for my 27 at Lord's in 1966. There was no doubt that they considered I'd come back from the dead in the nick of time. The phone in the dressing-room didn't stop ringing for an hour afterwards – and every call was for me. I just stood there with a glass of beer in my hand, laughing and joking with all my friends who called. I didn't feel any animosity to those who'd frustrated my progress, my main feeling was one of pleasure and accomplishment. Originally I'd batted for myself on that first day, but as my innings continued I was doing it for the non-whites in South Africa. I was still one of them and I was on my way back to them with an enhanced reputation.

On the Saturday, Doug Insole, in his capacity as chairman of the selectors, asked me if I was available for the tour. I took that as a good omen and a conversation later that day with Colin Cowdrey confirmed my optimism. He told me how well I'd done, that he was delighted I'd made a successful comeback and that in his opinion I ought to go on the tour. As captain of the side, he wanted to know what would be my feelings about playing at Newlands, at the Wanderers' stadium in Johannesburg, how would the media behave towards me. I think I reassured him; I said I wouldn't be making any press statements, that I would leave all that to the manager and captain and that I would be extremely careful about where I went throughout the tour. Colin said he would accept full responsibility for me and he would tell the England selectors so.

The rest of that Test held little interest for me; I couldn't wait for Wednesday, when the tour party was to be announced. After an amazing cloudburst on the final day, we had almost given up any hope of a resumption and the victory we deserved. But Colin said, 'We'll play by five o'clock, the water's just lying on the top. If we get the crowd to sweep it off with brooms and sticks, we'll be OK.' He was right and we had an hour to finish off the Aussies. That's when fate took another hand; after twenty minutes, nothing much had happened and I started pestering Colin for a bowl. I just felt I could break the stubborn stand between Jarman and Inverarity. At 5.25, Colin relented and in my first over, I bowled Jarman with one that just clipped the top off his stump as he tried to leave it alone. I'd done my stuff, Derek Underwood rolled the rest over, taking 7 for 50, and we just got home. It was a memorable match.

That evening, as I drove home, I idly mused about the other blokes that would be in the tour party. Little did I realize that at that time, a heart-searching debate was going on till 2 am among the selectors about my part in the proceedings.

The following day, I played against Sussex at Worcester. Just after six o'clock, I'd completed a carefree hundred when I told the Sussex lads, 'Bowl me a straight one and I'll get out. I want to listen to the tour party on the 6.30 radio news.' I skied one up in the air and got into the dressing-room just in time to hear the news summary. I kept waiting to hear my name in the list of players but it wasn't there. I was numbstruck. You could have heard a pin drop in the room. I don't know how long I stood there but the first thing I recall was Tom Graveney swearing bitterly and saying, 'I never thought they'd do that to you, Bas.' Tom saw the state I was in and he took me into the physio's room where I broke down and sobbed like a baby. Tom let me get away early and as I stepped outside the pavilion, I saw my son, Damian. 'Never mind, Dad,' he shouted, 'you're still the greatest.' I didn't feel it, I was like a zombie. The stomach had been kicked out of me. I remember thinking, 'You just can't beat the white South Africans', but I wasn't bitter. My mood was simply one of resignation, of desperate sadness.

When I got home I went upstairs and lay on a bed with my eyes closed for a few minutes. Then I looked up and saw Naomi. Just as she started to say something, I started crying. I sobbed my heart out while she whispered, 'Never mind, Bas, it'll all come right.' Then after half an hour, she said, 'Now what about a cup of tea?' I felt better for those private minutes upstairs and I could even see the funny side of things when I switched on the TV. The programme was 'Opportunity Knocks' and there was a white guy dressed up like a black man, singing Al Jolson songs.

I took Naomi out for a meal that night, resigned to the fact that the matter was now out of my hands and unaware that tons of newsprint condemning the England selectors were being assembled in Fleet Street printing presses for the next day's papers. Members of Parliament started kicking up a fuss, some MCC members resigned in protest and the row raged on for weeks. Within the space of four days, I received 2,000 letters, only one of which criticized me. One poor bloke from the Post Office had to report for work an hour early, simply to deal with my personal mail!

The reaction from well-wishers was wonderfully heartwarming but I was worried about how my family were being troubled by all the publicity. Naomi was badly affected – she went grey almost overnight, her skin looked bad, she was getting lower and lower in morale. My family couldn't walk down the road without newspaper placards reminding them of the D'Oliveira Affair. My youngest son, Shaun, was out with Naomi one day and although he couldn't read the placard, he saw our name. 'Mummy, has Daddy done anything wrong?' he asked.

Doug Insole said that I wasn't one of the 16 best players in England at that time, so I wasn't selected on purely cricketing grounds. I left it to the national press to state my case on cricketing grounds and I don't think I need add to their words.

Then I did something that enraged the South African Government; I accepted an invitation from the *News of the World* to cover the Tests in South Africa with the assistance of their cricket writer Peter Smith. Both Worcestershire and the MCC gave their blessing but Mr Vorster was suspicious. 'Guests who have ulterior motives or who are sponsored by people with ulterior motives usually find that they are not invited,' he said. He accused the *News of the World* of making political capital out of me. For my part, I couldn't see what all the fuss was about. To avoid any embarrassment, I wouldn't fly out with the England side, I wouldn't be seeking any facilities denied to other non-whites in South Africa and at close of play, I would give my comments to Peter Smith, who would write it all up. Nobody made a fuss about a similar arrangement involving Brian Close in the previous winter. He'd been sacked as England's captain, yet went on the tour to cover the series for a Fleet Street paper. Nobody talked about 'ulterior motives' then.

But soon my involvement with the *News of the World* was to prove academic. Tom Cartwright told the selectors he wasn't fit to tour and suddenly I was chosen to replace him. I didn't care about the fact that the selectors were now choosing me as an all-rounder when a fortnight earlier they'd justified their decision to exclude me by saying that I was being judged purely as a batsman, because my bowling wasn't penetrative enough overseas. That didn't matter anymore – the goal was again in sight and the well-wishers were again slapping me on the back. That marvellous feeling lasted about 24 hours. On Tuesday, September 17, Mr Vorster announced he was not prepared to accept the side. He described me as 'a political football'. So that was it. The dream had died. Again I felt sad and sorry for everyone who was innocent in this affair – the sportsmen, the spectators, the non-whites in South Africa who'd been so jubilant when they heard I was coming after all.

Was I sorry for myself? Of course, but, curiously, not as desperately as during those terrible, heart-rending few hours after the team had originally been announced and I wasn't in it. I'd done my best, nobody could surely reproach me. I realized that my original non-selection represented the best of both worlds for the Nationalist Government – there was no chance of me becoming a national hero on the cricket field, and the tour would implicitly put the seal of approval on the apartheid policies. I believe there would have been no trouble on that tour if I had gone. I was now accustomed to the need to uphold dignity and sportsmanship as often as I could and I knew that I could have helped change a few minds in South Africa and that a great chance was lost to show that people of all colours can co-exist peacefully. Perhaps Mr Vorster might have reacted differently if I'd been picked in the first place, if he hadn't been so enraged by the *News of the World* deal, if he hadn't been under great pressure from the right-wing of his party to take a stance which would still the gradual murmur of approval for multi-racial sport in South Africa. Perhaps, perhaps, perhaps.

Of course I was suspicious about various aspects of the saga but I lacked the inclination to try to get to the bottom of things. A lot of people outside the cricket world got sucked into the great big vacuum cleaner that constituted the D'Oliveira affair and a lot of them didn't know what the hell was going on. Many informed sources in the press thought that the South African Government put up the money for Tiene Oosthuizen to buy me off just before the Oval Test. I have no evidence of that, but it was a hell of a lot of money and why was he so keen to sign me up before the tour party was picked? Why did he cancel the international call once he'd heard I was playing at the Oval?

Lord Cobham is dead now but I never discussed his briefing session with Mr Vorster in which he gleaned the information that I was not welcome. But that information was, in my opinion, an extension of what I suspected, that political forces were at work. Sir Alec Douglas-Home offered the advice of an experienced politician and it differed to Lord Cobham's. I can't blame the MCC for agreeing with Sir Alec that it was best just to let the matter ride for a few months, to avoid forcing the hand of the South African Government. During my own personal crisis in September 1968 I visited Sir Alec at his flat and he was very disappointed at Mr Vorster's attitude. He was particularly worried that the Springbok tour scheduled for the UK in 1970 was in danger of being called off because he wanted the South African Government to see how their British counterparts could handle law-abiding demonstrations without resorting to violence to break them up.

I spent the night at Colin Cowdrey's home just after the tour was called off. He was terribly upset and was still hoping he could fly out on a peace mission to South Africa and save the tour at the last minute. I'm sure Colin voted for me at that fateful selectors' meeting – but strangely enough I've never bothered wondering how the other votes went. Such thoughts just seemed pointless. Colin cheered me up when he told me why he insisted that I should replace Roger Prideaux; Kent had played Surrey at the Oval the previous week on a wicket very near to the Test track. It was a flat wicket and the only bowler who got any real assistance from it was the Kent seamer Alan Dixon, who bowled at about the same pace as myself and kept beating the bat. Now Colin was always a great theorist and he filed that away in his mind. When Prideaux dropped out, Colin made the other selectors forget their alternatives and the skipper got his way. The rest is history.

Another forgotten man in the whole story is that fine all-rounder Barry Knight. Barry was very much a valued member of the England squad in 1968 and would surely have been a strong contender for the South African trip. But his personal life was giving him a few problems and just before the Leeds Test, an article under his name appeared in a Sunday paper. It was all pretty lurid – Barry said his marriage had broken up, he was expected to be declared bankrupt any day now and that he had contemplated suicide that season. Barry was made twelfth man at Leeds and he wasn't fit for the Oval Test. But it later emerged that for disciplinary reasons he would not be considered for the winter tour. If that article had not been published, surely Barry would have got in ahead of me in the tour party? And wouldn't he have played at the Oval instead of me if he'd been fit enough?

Tom Cartwright's injury; Roger Prideaux's pleurisy; Barry Knight's fitness and personal problems and Alan Dixon's seam bowling in a county match at the Oval. These were the links of circumstance in a chain of events that drove South Africa out of Test cricket. And you don't believe in fate?

7 A Year of Recovery

I eventually snapped out of my gloom after Mr Vorster shut the door on my dream. I realized I was a professional cricketer and the words of Sir Alec Douglas-Home kept recurring in my mind: 'Keep doing it out on the cricket field, that's your job. Other forces can look after events off the field.'

I still felt I had things to prove as a cricketer, not least that I was the best number six batsman England had, a fact that was obviously in doubt when the selectors picked the side for South Africa. I was due to go to Pakistan and Ceylon with England that winter, a trip that had been hastily arranged after the collapse of the South African tour, but, before then, I was scheduled to play in a double wicket competition organized by Datsun, the car company. This trip was offered to me after the South African tour was called off and I welcomed the chance to visit Australia for the first time and to battle on the cricket field with some old adversaries like Wes Hall, Bill Lawry, Bobby Simpson, Graham McKenzie and Rohan Kanhai. I was to partner Fred Trueman in the contest and Ken Barrington and Colin Milburn were also on the trip, so there was bound to be some fun.

But what I *really* wanted was to prove myself in competition with the South African players. Dennis Lindsay, Trevor Goddard, Graeme and Peter Pollock were all involved, and even though I had absolutely nothing against them as individuals, the events of August and September were still obviously fresh in my mind. I wanted to prove I could match them, so that it would make headlines and perhaps cause a ripple or two in the South African Government. I knew that would cause a hell of a lot more than a few ripples on Signal Hill and I grinned to myself as I thought about the reaction among my people if I played well. And I *did* play well. Fred and I did better than several more glamorous pairings, even though neither of us was exactly in the first flush of youth. And to my great delight, we even beat the Pollocks.

I knew what to expect from the media when I flew out to

Australia. The interviewers were much more aggressive than in England and, of course, they wanted to talk about South Africa. I took my time and explained patiently that at the moment I was only concerned with cricket; after that things were fine. I loved the Australian people and quickly learned that their style of speech was in fact nowhere near as hostile and insulting as it sounded.

I knew that relations with the South Africans might have been a little tense and I shall always be grateful to Dennis Lindsay for breaking the ice. He said he was very sorry on behalf of the South African nation and the others quickly followed suit. After that, we were just cricketers in each others' eyes and it made me realize that it was an odd world as I sat watching South Africa's Pollock brothers taking on West Indies' Kanhai and Griffith in a match. We all wished the same players could face up to each other in a Test Match.

That fine fast bowler, Peter Pollock, also buried the hatchet with me over a row that had festered for a couple of years. At the end of the 1966 season, I had been playing in a festival game at Scarborough and Peter Pollock was on the opposing side. Now Pollock was a very aggressive quickie, a typical South African in fact. Well, he bowled me a beamer in this game at Scarborough and the crowd – that lovely Yorkshire crowd who always supported me loudly – all went mad. I wasn't too keen either. I was prepared to give him the benefit of the doubt, to think that the ball had slipped or that his footholds were troubling him – but no, he just looked straight at me grimly, didn't apologize or look at his footholds. All the anger and frustration of a coloured South African facing up to a white South African welled up inside me and I thought, 'I'll get you'. I didn't believe he would bowl another beamer at me so I decided to hit him out of sight next ball. Fortunately the ball pitched in just the right spot and I can still see it flying into the top of the stand and the crowd cheering themselves hoarse. I slogged another four off him before the end of the over and then he walked past me without saying a word. The captain, Bobby Simpson, walked past me and said, 'I'd better take him off'. I said, 'Don't do that, leave him on, I'm enjoying it.' Well, the same thing went on for a couple more overs and I kept slogging him. He never apologized and the blacks in

South Africa loved it when they heard I'd hit the white South African for six. I wasn't too displeased either.

Anyway, two years later, I asked all the Datsun competitors into my hotel room for drinks and all the South African players were there. Peter started to apologize for Scarborough 1966, saying that he didn't mean to bowl me a beamer, that it was a mistake, etc, etc. I said, 'Do you honestly expect me to believe that? It's taken you two years to apologize.' Peter insisted he didn't mean it and I said 'OK forget it' and thought no more about it. We've become great friends since, and he's a very intelligent guy who believes sincerely in multi-racial sport in South Africa. Mind you, he still showed a little bit of devil on that Datsun trip. Fred and I played against the Pollock brothers at Perth, at that time the fastest wicket in the world. Peter was bowling at Fred and he sent down a vicious bouncer; Fred just got the bat handle up to the ball and deflected it over the slips for a boundary. Fred came down the wicket and asked what the hell was going on. Peter replied, 'Don't worry, Fred, we've got to show the crowd this is a genuine game of cricket, that we're all trying.' Fred accepted that and Peter agreed to give him a signal when he was going to bowl the next bouncer. The next ball was another bouncer – minus the signal! Fred went absolutely berserk, saying, 'I'll meet you another time, another place', and I don't think they've been all that friendly ever since.

We were all treated magnificently by Datsun on that tour and the credit for that goes to a man who, I believe, was the forerunner of Kerry Packer. His name was Jack Neary. He was in the theatrical business and he was taken on to present and package the product for the Australian public. He made certain all the players had anything they wanted, we stayed at the best hotels and the money was excellent. Jack realized that the old-style promotion just wasn't enough, and some of Kerry Packer's bright and breezy ideas a decade later were straight out of the Jack Neary handbook. I don't know what happened to him, but not one of the players on that trip will forget him.

An incident at Melbourne, however, cast a shadow over what was a highly enjoyable fortnight. Ken Barrington suffered a heart-attack in the dressing-room and retired from cricket as a result. The strain of carrying England's batting for

years just got to him. The throwing controversy was also getting him down; he'd made it quite clear in print that, in his
opinion, Charlie Griffith threw the occasional delivery. Charlie
wasn't happy about the allegation and, as luck would have it,
the two players came up against each other in a Datsun match.
Well, Ken and Colin Milburn had just beaten Griffith and
Kanhai in their match. That was a surprise and what was even
more surprising was that the two West Indians hadn't yet won
a match. They were annoyed at themselves and also complained bitterly about the fielders. They kept saying that the
fielders took brilliant catches for the Englishmen but didn't do
the same for the West Indians. Ken said, 'All I can say lads, is
bad luck and I hope it evens itself out next time.' There was
obviously some tension between Charlie and Ken about the
throwing allegations and Charlie kept going on about everything that displeased him at that time. The next thing we
knew was that Ken was starting to sweat profusely in the dressing room. I said, 'You'd better lie down, mate', and Fred and
I went out to play our match. A few minutes later the loudspeaker asked for a doctor and I later learned that Ken had
been whisked off to hospital with a heart attack. It was a sad
and sour end to a great career. I couldn't get into the state that
Ken found himself in during a Test; he'd be up early in the
morning, drinking tea, smoking and pacing the floor nerv-
ously. But I felt for him and always admired his dedication,
technique, professionalism and utter pride at batting for England. He suffered agonies for England; he used to look so
intense as he sat on the players' balcony waiting to bat. If anyone ever tells you that Ken Barrington didn't give all that
much for England, look up his Test record and point out what
it did to his health.

The tragedy of Ken Barrington was a sobering thought to
take with me as I prepared to re-enter the Test Match fray.
With due respect to Pakistan, I knew that this hastily-arranged
trip involving three Tests couldn't compare with the South
African tour. All the players who've been to South Africa tell
me that it's the best England tour of them all, and knowing
the climate, the hospitality and the fast wickets, I was sure this
was the case. But it was good to be representing England
again and the way I was treated by my team-mates helped to

appease the sadness I felt at being the cause of missing such a great tour. They'd rib me about being the bloke who stopped the tour and I'd tell Roger Prideaux it was all his fault because he dropped out with illness. It was very good-humoured stuff and to be honest we needed a sense of humour on that trip to Pakistan.

At the height of the D'Oliveira Affair, there was much talk about 'keeping politics out of sport'. I agreed with that principle but knew it was naive to stick to it; my own case proved that, as did certain events in the Mexico Olympics of that year. In any case, it was becoming clear that sport was getting more and more important to the prestige of countries – Britain even had a Sports Minister. So sport and politics were inextricably linked as far as I could see, and the events of the Pakistan tour confirmed that in my mind. Student riots caused the abandonment of the Third Test at Karachi; they were demonstrating at the rule of martial law imposed by the country's president, Ayub Khan, and throughout the trip, there was an uneasy, rumbling sensation that we were sitting on a powder keg.

A couple of days before the First Test at Lahore, I attended a reception with the rest of the England team. I was asked to meet a pleasant, well-mannered man. He was one of the student's leaders and I was impressed with his intelligence and his grasp of the outside world. He said, 'It's a great pleasure to meet you. I admired your behaviour during the recent traumas. South Africa is a bad country, things must change over there.' He said that if he ever became President of Pakistan, he would invite me back as his special guest. He mentioned that he played cricket and I asked if the Pakistan side had been picked yet. 'No,' he replied, 'but I know *I'm* playing. If I don't play, there's no Test Match.' His name was Aftab Gul. Later, during the riots, I saw his power over the demonstrators. He just put up his hands like a gladiator and everybody sat down and kept quiet.

We didn't mind his selection, because he wasn't much of a batsman. He toured England twice in 1971 and 1974 and never made it in Test cricket – but it was fascinating to realize that politics played such an important part in Pakistan cricket. That little chat with Aftab Gul only confirmed me in my view that I was right to concentrate on my cricket on that tour. Before we flew out from England, I had decided I wasn't going to make the same mistake as in the West Indies. I might be snowed under with invitations from well-meaning people but it was important for me to devote my attention to cricket this time. I had to regain the ground I'd lost in the West Indies.

The First Test was a dreary, drawn affair with Colin Cowdrey delaying his declaration and the Pakistanis giving up the ghost early on. For me it was more fascinating for events off the field featuring that strong-willed, erratic character, John Snow. Before the team was announced, he was messing about in the nets, bowling left-arm and waiting to bowl at John Edrich. Tom Graveney was in charge of the session and when the BBC's cricket correspondent, Brian Johnston, turned up with a Pakistani camerman who wanted to take some film of the England players, Tom readily agreed. Not surprisingly, the little Pakistani wanted some news film of John Snow, because he was a big star after his exploits in the West Indies – and after all you don't get many quick bowlers in Pakistan. Well, Snowy didn't want to know and Tom said, 'Come on, do the bloke a favour, come in off your long run.' Snowy did so reluctantly, the film was shot and the Pakistani was fulsome in his gratitude. Unfortunately there was something wrong with his camera and he asked if he could take Snowy again off his long run; by this time our fast bowler was livid but Tom made him go back off his long run and go through the motions with John Edrich.

Anyway, it was the morning of the Test and we were all in the dressing-room. Cowdrey went over to Snowy and said, 'John, I want you to be twelfth man – I don't think the wicket will favour you.' All went quiet, we felt as if a bomb was about to explode. Snowy went on with his duties, put on his blazer and walked out with a face like thunder. He showed what he thought of Cowdrey's decision during the lunch interval when he was nowhere to be seen. Cowdrey sent for him and told him he had to bring out the drinks in the afternoon session – sure enough, Snowy did so, wearing his England blazer and his whites, but with a pair of flip-flop sandals on! The press and TV loved it and Snowy felt he'd made his protest. He clearly blamed Tom Graveney and the incident with the cameraman for his dropping, and when we got to Dacca for the next Test he got his own back on Tom. The practice wickets were terribly dangerous and Snowy mucked around bowling left-armers until Tom came in to the net. Straightaway, Snowy reverted to his long run and pinged some really fierce bouncers round Tom's ears. There was clearly a bit of needle there and again the media had a field day.

Soon we were on our way to Dacca and in fear of our lives. The students threatened all sorts of mayhem, yet the British Ambassador made it clear to us that we'd be in no danger, that all was peaceful and that there'd be greater trouble if we called off the Test because the rioters were cricket-mad. Two nights before the Second Test, we were at a reception given by the Ambassador. All was going well and amicably when we happened to notice some white people pass by the window. That was a fairly rare sight in Dacca, yet they didn't come into the party. I thought no more of it and then after an hour, we were asked to move to another room. No problem. After a few minutes of idle banter we saw another group of whites pass the window and they too disappeared from sight. Then we were asked if we minded moving to another house. By that time we didn't care where the hell we went and we were amused when this chap was got out of bed and told by the Ambassador that he had to entertain us. Things went well for about an hour until I plucked up courage to ask the host about all the white people walking around outside. 'Don't you know?' he said. 'They've come for the air-lift.' All the British in the area were being air-lifted out of Dacca because of the threat of civil disorder, yet we were expected to stay and play cricket with the rioters looking on!

Things were getting odder and odder. The next day we had a look at the wicket. It was a stirring sight – all the brains of English cricket sniffing and prodding and coming up with different conclusions. David Brown seemed to have the best idea; he'd played there two years previously with the England Under-25 side and he said it would play like a Jamaican wicket. It certainly *looked* a quick bowler's wicket, flat, shiny and dark brown. So the selectors decided on a three-man seam attack, with just one spinner, Derek Underwood. Morale was high in the dressing-room on the morning of the match because we felt we had a well-balanced attack. Cowdrey came in, looking extremely disconsolate – 'I've lost the toss, lads,' he said. Well, that's happened before, we thought, what's he so glum about? 'I have to tell you something,' he said. 'We've picked three seamers and one spinner, right? They've picked four spinners and just one seamer.' I thought, 'When in Rome, etc. Somebody's made a hell of a mistake and I hope it's not us.' The first ball from John Snow skidded through to Alan Knott who took it down by his ankles and by the end of the over, a bloody great hole had appeared in the wicket. So much for Brown's Jamaican wicket!

They battled through to 246, which was a good total, even though our attack wasn't suited to a wicket that was a paradise for the spinners. By the second day, the wicket was a complete shambles; there was nothing underneath the top soil, the whole of the crust had gone and it was a mudheap. The ball was starting to behave extraordinarily and we all thought we'd be doing miraculously if we got to 120, even with master craftsmen like Cowdrey and Graveney in the side. I was in at the close and the ball was getting lower and lower so that I thought I would need a shovel. Just before the close, I enjoyed one of those slices of luck that everyone needs; Saeed Ahmed bowled an off-break, I pushed forward and it went up in the air off bat and pad. A complete dolly, if you'll pardon the pun, except that short leg and the bowler just looked at each other and waited for the other one to take the gift. It plopped to the ground, I said 'Thank you very much', and managed to hold out till close of play with England about 130 for 7 and me on 12 or so. It was a good total in the circumstances.

That night we were at a party (tea and cakes, it *was* Pakistan, after all) and I was chatting to John Thicknesse, the cricket writer of the London *Evening Standard*. Now Thickers is a good lad, a forthright character who used to upset people with some of his articles, but I've no doubts that he genuinely loves cricket and the players. Well before we arrived in Pakistan he'd told me that he thought the selectors were right to omit me from the South African party. He thought I wasn't one of the best 16 cricketers in the English bag and he wrote this in his paper, creating quite a hue and cry. I thanked him for telling me this and told him not to worry about any recriminations from me about his sincere opinions. 'Just one thing I want you to promise me, Thickers,' I said on the plane. 'If you change your mind after my performances out in Pakistan, will you say so in print and show me your article?' He said he'd be only too pleased.

So Thickers and I were chatting at Dacca as England were really in the cart. 'How are we going to get out of it tomorrow, Basil?' he asked. 'They lead by over a hundred and you've only got the tail to keep you company – and what about that wicket?' By this time, I was feeling fairly jaunty and said, 'Don't worry about it, Thickers, I'll get a hundred tomorrow.' Of course I didn't mean that, anyone who got to twenty on that track had done pretty well. We bet each other a pint of beer that I'd score a hundred and parted the best of friends. The next morning, as I was having a net, Thickers came up to me and said, 'Have you seen that wicket, Bas? It's got worse.' 'No', I answered, 'I don't want to see the wicket, I'll get a hundred, Thickers, you'll see.' It was sheer bravado, but by this time I felt I had to keep up the pretence.

But I *did* get a hundred and it was the greatest innings of my life. My partners only had to face one or two balls an over, I slogged the ball for boundaries whenever possible, blocked the good deliveries and breathed a sigh of relief when the ball turned so much that it missed the stumps. This was against two leg-spinners, Intikhab and Mushtaq, an off-spinner, Saeed Ahmed, and a slow left-armer, Pervez Sajjad, on a wicket with no top. All the time, the Pakistani close fielders kept saying to me, 'You're not English, you're one of us. If you get out we can beat them.' I just laughed and carried on, enjoying the struggle and thinking about Thickers' face. I scored 114 not out in out total of 274 and I was so proud. That night I was lying in a hot bath in my hotel room, savouring the moment and my achievement. John Thicknesse knocked on the door and my room-mate, John Murray, showed him into the bathroom. 'Well played, Bas', he said. 'Now why can't you do that for Worcestershire more often?' I could have brained him – there I was, thousands of miles from Worcester, having played the greatest innings of my life and he said that. He was as good as his word and printed a nice piece about my innings in the *Evening Standard,* but I never got my pint off him.

The game ended in a draw when Colin Cowdrey decided to go on the defensive once they batted again. I think he was worried about facing a struggle on the last afternoon, with the pitch getting even worse. An opportunity lost – but at least I had the consolation of proving myself in Test cricket.

So to Karachi and a two-day Test. Riots stopped play after England scored 500 and we flew home – but not before Alan Knott had tried valiantly to get his first Test century. He was 96 not out when it became clear that the students were about to come over the fences. The Pakistan President was at the match and they obviously realized that stopping a Test would make world-wide news. David Brown was at the non-striker's end and Knotty was begging Intikhab to toss up a dolly so he could get his century. It was getting worse all the time and suddenly David Brown shouted, 'I'm off' and sprinted for safety. They tore down the main stand and set it alight; it was like Kingston all over again.

Colin Milburn had already managed a hundred before the rioters took over; he'd been flown out to replace the injured Roger Prideaux and in this innings, Colin really came of age as a Test batsman. It was a very restrained, responsible knock and, at the time, I thought that this was just the start of a great Test career for Colin. Unfortunately, he lost an eye within a few months of that innings and he was never the same again. A lot of people say he would have struggled in limited over cricket because of his bulk but I'm sure he could have been hidden somewhere. I was for several years, after all. I realize he would only have lasted till he was about 35, due to his size – but he *was* only 27 at the time of his car crash. I think Geoff Boycott is the only current England player who's better than the Colin Milburn of 1969. At that stage, Colin was starting to put the whole thing together, to restrain himself ever so slightly, but he could still hit the ball out of sight. Colin was a loss not only to the spectators but also to the players. He was the kind of bloke you wanted to do well – for the sake of the game as well as himself.

I returned to England to find my Test career continuing in 1969 under another new captain – Ray Illingworth. He had no official experience apart from a few weeks with his new county, Leicestershire, but anyone who'd played against the great Yorkshire team under Brian Close knew how much Ray had to offer in tactical appreciation. That 1969 England side was going through a transitional period and Ray did wonders holding it together. Admittedly our position wasn't exceptionally taxing but it's a captain's job to make the best of his resources and Ray was magnificent at that. One particular incident in the Leeds Test against the West Indies convinced me he had all the necessary qualities of leadership. They had to get just over 300 to win and, at 219 for 3, they were running away with it. The time was 5.45, Basil Butcher was well set, Clive Lloyd was feeling his way and Gary Sobers was next man in. It was obviously a crucial time for both sides. I walked past a pensive Ray and said, 'What do you think, then?' He replied, 'If we break this partnership before 6.15, we've got a great chance of winning. If we don't, then we've lost it.' In the next over, Butcher gloved one to Knott behind the stumps. In came Sobers and straight away, the skipper brought back Barry Knight. He'd worked out that Gary was slightly vulnerable to a bowler of Barry's pace; a back-foot player was often surprised by Barry's nip off the wicket. Anyway, he ran in and bowled the delivery we all wanted to see – just outside the off-stump and hurrying through. Sobers went to play it, was surprised by the speed and he dragged it on to his stumps. Shortly afterwards, Lloyd faced up to the new bowler, Illingworth, who bowled a slightly quicker one which Lloyd nicked to Knott. Within a quarter of an hour, they had lost the match, due to Ray's astute bowling changes and resolution in carrying out his plans. Even more significantly, he knew just how much time the match would be hanging in the balance – only thirty minutes.

The 1969 West Indians weren't a great side. They relied far too much on Gary Sobers and with his knee beginning to trouble him, he was just a shadow of his former self. There were other sad moments in that series – Tom Graveney took a decision that he knew might end his Test career. It was his benefit season and he decided to play in a Sunday match, even though he was forbidden to do so by the England selectors. He knew what he was doing and presumably, at 41, he realized his days were numbered at Test level and that the £1,000 he picked up for the Sunday game was preferable to the £120 Test Match fees that would soon dwindle away in his case. Whatever the rights and wrongs, the England team lost a great batsman when we could least afford it – and the following season, Tom retired from first-class cricket.

However, it looked as if England had found an ideal replacement for Tom in the Second Test at Lord's when Jackie Hampshire made a century on his debut. That was a magnificent knock, with class oozing out of the lad. But he lasted just one more Test and then was dropped for some reason. I was amazed at the decision because it opened the way for several batsmen who just weren't in Hampshire's class. And when you've scored a hundred at Lord's in your first Test, surely you should get more than one other Test before you're dropped. If Jackie Hampshire had played for the rest of the Test matches in that summer, he could have been a England regular for a decade. The whims of the selectors . . .

A couple of other memories from those 1969 Tests – Geoff Boycott getting disturbed both by Gary Sobers' late swing with the new ball, the aggression and hostility of New Zealand's Dick Motz, and my first sight of a young man who was soon to make hundreds of runs for my county, Glenn Turner. In 1969, Boycott simply had a mediocre Test summer by his standards. He'd opted for contact lenses and he took some time adjusting to things, but he fought back in subsequent years and made the cynics eat their words. Good luck to Boycott, he's been written off more times than he's scored hundreds. Another man with almost the same hunger for runs as Boycott was Glenn Turner. But first he had to learn the English game and when I saw him carry his bat throughout the New Zealand innings at Lord's with Derek Underwood in full cry, I thought, 'This bloke can play'. He wasn't scoring all that much but he was staying in and watching everything on to the bat. His defence was immaculate and although I thought he would always remain a blocker, he proved me wrong when he came to Worcester and blossomed into a really fine, attractive player.

Boycott wasn't the only England batsman to have a poor Test summer. I was out of sorts all the time. I just couldn't get going at any level of the game and failed to reach 1,000 runs in first-class cricket. I suppose it was just a reaction to the events of the previous couple of years. I felt, though, that I was entitled to one bad season, even though I realized that my age and lack of a sound technique would eventually take its toll and affect my performances. At that time, I particularly wished I had the overall technique of a Cowdrey or a Graveney. They could play till their fifties if they felt like it because they were so straight and immaculate.

But I still loved playing for England and I was looking forward to the 1970 season. The South Africans were due.

8 1970-The Rest of the World Series

I shed no tears when the 1970 Springbok tour to the UK was called off by the Government because of fears of public disorder. I disagreed with plans to disrupt the matches – after all, once you're playing, it seems unfair to spoil things – but I agreed that the anti-apartheid campaigners were right to try to get the tour halted. I thought a dose of sporting isolation would do South Africa some good, it would make their politicians realize things were wrong in the eyes of most of the free world.

I'm sure the Nationalist Government was delighted when the MCC initially stated that the 1970 tour would go ahead. Mr Vorster and co. no doubt thought such an offer would look good in the eyes of the electorate; it more or less sanctioned apartheid. It was no use pleading that politics and sport shouldn't mix – those who had that glib catch-phrase to hand should have been on my tour to Pakistan. South Africa was terrified of losing its links with the MCC and when the tour was called off, they were happy to blame it on left-wingers, Communists and general loonies – which was an insult to fair-minded men like Peter Hain, Dennis Brutus, Mike Brearley, the Rev David Sheppard and John Arlott.

By this time, I was stepping away from the limelight over race relations. I was happy to leave the campaigning to articulate, able and sincere men like Brutus and Hain. I told Brutus, 'Use what I'm doing on the cricket field for your campaign, but don't pull me this way and that for public statements.' The thing was moving along and the events of the previous two years meant that more and more politically-aware people were taking up the correct public stance in my opinion. I felt I should simply continue doing my job, to carry the banner for non-racialism on the cricket field. It was up to the white cricketers of South Africa to take up their case with the one man whose decision inevitably led to the cancellation of the 1970 tour – Mr Vorster. I had decided I would play against the Springboks if they toured England – it would have meant apartheid in reverse if I'd stepped down. But I wanted South Africa's whites to hammer at the Government's door.

Some misjudged my stance, and I can't blame them. Some Cape Coloureds who were living in England at that time wrote to me saying I was insensitive and unthinking about racial issues, that I should come out against the Springbok tour. That annoyed me so much that I wrote back to them. 'I agree with everything you wrote,' I replied. 'Now can I make a suggestion? Because our people are suffering so much in South Africa, I suggest we all leave Britain and take our families back to South Africa. Will all of you who have signed this letter come back with the D'Oliveira family? I will if you will.' To this day, I have never received a reply. They were happy to shout the odds and suggest I was coasting along, oblivious to my own people's needs. I maintain I suffered more than they could ever have known because of my colour.

I didn't feel bitter towards the South Africans included in the hastily-arranged Rest of the World tour party. The Pollock brothers were included, Barry Richards, Mike Procter and Eddie Barlow. But I must admit I found something stirring inside me when I came up against them on the cricket field. And I'm sure they had the same feelings because it's not easy to change overnight. We'd lived in a society that told us where to go, who to live with, who we could make love to and what to believe in – all determined by Government policy. Growing up with all that, it was inevitable that emotions would bubble near the surface when I came up against the white stars on the cricket field. I got on very well with them at close of play but I kept thinking – if only I'd had the chance to play good quality cricket at the same age as you blokes. Then you might have seen something.

I thought the Rest of the World series was a good idea. We wanted international cricket in England, not just for the revenue involved but also because the top players needed regular match practice at the highest level. And this was the highest level, I assure you; this series apparently doesn't count in official Test records but it certainly felt like the authentic stuff. It was one of the hardest series I have ever played in. Some of the opposition were a little rusty after missing out for several months but we were up against class. Procter was coming in at number nine, Intikhab batted at ten in one game and their middle-order batting revolved round Kanhai, Pollock, Lloyd and Sobers. The white South Africans obviously had a lot to prove to the fans and the West Indians didn't want to be over-shadowed by anybody – and they tell me it wasn't the real thing!

In the first match at Lord's, Gary Sobers bowled like a demon to hustle us out cheaply. It was a little damp and he took six wickets with some lovely late swing. Then he went in and absolutely murdered the bowling for 183. He played like a true genius and obviously the presence of so many great play-ers made him raise his game to prove just who *was* the number one. Nearly 600 runs and 21 wickets at the end of the series were his answer.

In our second innings, Ray Illingworth and I put on over a hundred but the ball was starting to turn and Intikhab's leg-spin was too much. Ray just missed out on his century; it was about this time that he started to blossom as an authentic number six batsman. He worked away at his batting, cut out the flashy shots and finished the series with nearly 500 runs, more than any other England player.

So we were one down by the time we got to the next game at Trent Bridge. Tony Greig made his debut – big, glamorous, confident and a great crowd-puller. I loved playing with Greigy, he would try like hell and could always share a laugh when the game was over. He took seven wickets in the match in humid conditions ideal for our swing bowlers. I even picked up seven wickets and at one stage had the chance of an illustrious hat-trick. I got Kanhai caught by Knott, then had Graeme Pollock LBW. In walked Clive Lloyd and I thought to myself, 'has anybody ever picked up three such players in suc-cession?' Unfortunately Clive met my first ball plumb in the middle of the bat.

Eddie Barlow was another South African to do well in that match. He took five wickets in the first innings and bowled me with a delivery that came back like a snake. A very underrated bowler, he never gave up. He knew he was slightly short of the highest class but he'd come on the field with the attitude, 'never mind the Kanhais, the Sobers and the Pollocks – I'm the greatest player here and don't you forget it.'

On the final day at Trent Bridge, the weather cleared, the wicket rolled out easy and with Brian Luckhurst scoring an unbeaten hundred in his second international match (if we can't call it a Test) we coasted home by eight wickets. Not a bad performance against a team like that.

I scored a hundred in the next game at Edgbaston and in the process won a psychological battle with Mike Procter. Now he's a hell of a sight as he comes tearing in off a long run and bowls off the wrong foot. In those days, he was really quick – he'd just helped destroy Australia with Peter Pollock's assistance and he was as sharp as anyone in the world. I miscued one hook, it bounced just short of mid-wicket and Procter stood there and said, 'You can't hook.' I said nothing, just tended the pitch and waited my turn. The next over he bounced me again and the ball flew into the stand. I said, 'Well, you're not all that quick anyway.' He finished up with five wickets in the innings and I got my hundred, so both of us were happy. And I nearly got my second hundred in the match – I was on 81 when I pushed forward to Gary Sobers. The ball turned and I nicked it to slip. By this time, the ball was starting to turn with Sobers, Gibbs and Intikhab sending down nearly 160 overs in the second innings. But we only left them 140-odd to win and despite a few alarms, Procter steered them home.

We were unlucky not to win the fourth match at Leeds. After being bowled out cheaply first time round, we fought back magnificently to leave them needing just over 200 to win. At one stage they were 62 for 5 but Sobers steadied things for a time. With two wickets to fall, Procter was joined by Barry Richards, who had ricked his back. As soon as he came in, it seemed to me that Barry gave the biggest bat/pad catch you've ever heard to Keith Fletcher at short leg. But he was given not out and we couldn't believe it. Knotty said, 'But you hit that, Barry'. Yet he stayed at the crease. If he'd been given out, there was only Lance Gibbs to come and forty runs to get.

So we went to the Oval 3–1 down, but in reality the honours should have been even. I saw only the first couple of days of the final game because I was made twelfth man. The selectors, with the tour of Australia in mind, wanted to have yet another look at Dennis Amiss, so I had to stand down. We lost by four wickets after setting them nearly 300 in the last knock, but with a batting order like theirs, they always had the upper hand. My abiding memory from that match is a partnership between two great left-handers that for political reasons will never be repeated. Graeme Pollock and Gary Sobers added over 150 and it was spell-binding stuff. But if you'd walked into the Oval that day and didn't know who was batting, you would have thought Pollock was the greater batsman. Of course, Sobers had overshadowed everybody else in that series while Graeme had struggled, but on this occasion the star was the South African.

One little incident I can recount from this match will, I hope, prove that even the great players have their doubts about their skills. Barry Richards hadn't done all that well, considering his great gifts, and on top of that he had back trouble. At the Oval, when I was twelfth man, I walked into the opposition dressing-room where he was having treatment. He looked up and said, 'Bas, how the hell do you people get runs in Test Matches?' This from the man who'd averaged 72 against the Aussies just a few months earlier. The great players also have self-doubts . . . but they're great *because* they fight back and re-assert themselves.

But my abiding memory of that 1970 series concerns the genius of Gary Sobers. A year earlier, he'd been a painful sight as he hobbled round England with a poor West Indies side. But the challenge of playing with so many great cricketers helped him to raise his game and he dominated the series. One remark of his that year summed up his mental attitude perfectly. At Leeds, the Rest of the World side had to graft to scrape home by two wickets. Gary made a half-century that, by his standards, was scratchy; Ray Illingworth beat him several times and he looked almost human. Over a drink afterwards I said I'd never seen him play and miss so much against Ray. And he said, 'You must get it right, Bas. I didn't play and miss – *he* missed me.' Only a genius with great self-belief could talk that way.

It had been a cracking good series in my opinion. The aggregate should have been 3–2 to them, not 4–1. We were excellently led by our captain, Ray Illingworth – and in the next few months, his leadership proved even more valuable.

9 The Ashes Regained 1970-1

I was too old to tour Australia when I did. The large grounds found me wanting, I had to struggle to get round. I had a good tour with the bat, though, and I think I justified Ray Illingworth's faith in me. He was magnificent on that tour; the press called us 'Dad's Army' and with three players pushing forty and a few others in their thirties, we weren't exactly spring lambs. But Ray nursed us along, with an uncanny ability to make use of all his resources, slender or otherwise. A classic example of that came on the last day of the Final Test at Sydney; we were without our best batsman, Boycott, and our best bowler, Snow, through injury, but Ray pulled the strings at the right time and we snatched a magnificent win. He backed us to the hilt to the press and would never admit publicly that any of us had let him down. But in private, he'd give anybody who deserved it a real roasting. We respected him for his loyalty and it was second nature that we should return it.

It was a difficult tour personally for Ray. He didn't get on very well with the manager, David Clark, and Colin Cowdrey wasn't involved enough as vice-captain; Colin was disappointed that he'd missed out on the captaincy on his fifth tour of Australia and that was reflected in his play. He seemed to go right into his shell and became very introspective off the field and with the bat. Strangely enough, he and I became even closer on that tour – perhaps the traumas of recent years acted as a bond between us.

The team was written off at the start but that didn't bother us in the slightest. We felt that there was no point in showing too much too soon and we eased our way through the early matches. One player was at the top of his form very early on – Geoff Boycott. In the first state game of the tour at Adelaide, he was not out 170-odd overnight and I said to Ray that the way things were going, only the first three batsmen would get a bat in the early matches. Ray saw the point and next day told Boycott, 'Play a few shots, we want a few more batters to have a knock today.' He was out quickly, caught down the leg-side by the keeper. He hadn't thrown his wicket away but he was furious that the hint had been dropped. He didn't speak to Ray for a couple of days, presumably feeling he could have got 300 on that perfect wicket. Ray, rightly, ignored him and Boycs came round. He continued making stacks of runs and we came to the Queensland match just before the First Test with some of us still a little short of match practice. Boycs asked Ray what he should do; he replied, 'You know what I want.' Boycs said he wasn't going to give his wicket away, that offended his professional pride. So he retired hurt officially, with a little matter of 124 to his name.

The First Test ended in stalemate; even at that early stage, Ray was formulating his plan – to hold things quietly together at Brisbane and Perth and press for a win at Sydney or Melbourne where the conditions sometimes favour the bowlers. In this First Test, Keith Stackpole made a fine double hundred after he was run out by a mile with his score at 18. The umpire was Lou Rowan, a former policeman – a combination guaranteed to get under the skin of that great anti-authority man, John Snow! He and Rowan never got on during that series.

I'd heard a lot about the barracking from the Aussie crowd and one wag at Brisbane didn't let me down. It was very hot, the Aussies were about 400 for 3 and this bloke on the boundary's edge kept telling me our side were hopeless. The flies were also irritating me and I was swatting them furiously when he shouted, 'Dolly, we're going to hammer you and you won't score any runs – and what's more, I want you to leave our bloody flies alone!'

We went on to Perth where the good folk of Western Australia staged their first-ever Test – and beautifully organized it was, too. They'd always wanted a Test out there and they tried their best to please everybody – even down to spraying the stadium with fly repellent every morning! Unfortunately the cricket on the final day wasn't all that stimulating – the Aussies didn't attempt the target of 245 in 2½ hours – but there was some fine play on previous days. I saw one of the fastest spells of bowling in my life in this game. John Snow had coasted through the tour so far under Illingworth's shrewd leadership but now he really slipped himself. For an hour there was only one fielder in front of the wicket – me. I was only there to collect the ball from Knotty and lob it back to the bowler. Knotty stood about forty yards back from the stumps and even then the ball was still rising as he took it. Doug Walters seemed almost frightened by Snowy and he often finished on his knees with his bat up in the air like a periscope. After two successive deliveries that went through at throat height, Lou Rowan warned Snowy for bowling too many bouncers. 'They're not bouncers – your batsmen just can't play them, that's all,' he answered. But Rowan warned him and told the skipper, who backed up Snowy and said the batsmen just weren't capable of playing short-pitched bowling. The next over from Snowy he bowled the most magnificent bouncer – and he turned round to Rowan and said, 'Now that *is* a bloody bouncer!'

Brian Luckhurst got a fine hundred in this Test. He was a very underrated player who didn't look all that special but worked at his game in county cricket and found a style of play that made him good runs at Test level. A nice chap, always with a kind word and a smile for everyone, he was a vital member of that solid batting order. Boycott, Luckhurst and Edrich weren't flashy players who could rattle up two-hour hundreds, but by God, they were a re-assuring sight when you were sweating it out in the dressing-room!

The only batsman on the Aussie side who was really technically correct was Ian Redpath. He'd been coached by Frank Tyson and it showed – bat and pad together, good shots through the covers, a solid player who took some winkling out. A more spectacular batsman was young Greg Chappell. He made a hundred against us on his debut in Tests and a handsome innings it was. Mind you, we played into his hands. Ray had worked out the line to bowl at him – just outside the off stump to tempt him to work it through the leg-side. If we bowled at the stumps, we knew he would murder us through mid-wicket. Ray got very annoyed at Ken Shuttleworth as Chappell kept whipping him through the field on the leg-side. 'Where the hell are you bowling?' he asked. 'I can't help what he's doing – I'm bowling outside the off-stump,' he said. Knotty confirmed to Ray that he was in fact bowling at the stumps and Ray barked, 'I know where he's bowling – that's why it's going on the leg-side!' Nevertheless, it was a fine knock by a man who's become a great Test batsman. He plays the ball very late and is a beautiful driver. I still maintain that you should bowl just outside his off-stump, though. Ask Ray Illingworth.

I had some lovely by-play in that Test with my old mate, Johnny Gleeson. I always had trouble picking his googly and he knew it, but this day I was batting really well when he bowled me with a huge full toss. I was livid with myself as I walked out and Johnny grinned at me, 'I always said you couldn't pick my wrong 'un'. A super bloke, he played his cricket as if it was 1910 all over again – 'I'm bloody glad to be here and I'm going to enjoy it' was his attitude. I wish there were more Gleesons around.

At this stage of the tour, I found myself with a new room-mate. He was Bob Willis, a very tall, gangling lad from Surrey who apparently bowled very fast. Alan Ward had broken down with shin trouble and John Edrich had told the management that young Willis might be a good bet to replace him. He had very little county experience and there wasn't much meat on his tall frame. But he bowled very fast once he got acclimatized to everything and it geed up John Snow just when he wanted that. When Snowy saw this lad charging in, making the ball rear up, he made a point of looking to his laurels and the only losers were the Aussie batsmen.

Bob settled in very quickly under my harsh, dictatorial tutelage. He'd bring me cups of coffee when I wanted, order breakfast and ask me endless questions about cricket. He was a quiet, unassuming lad with a good cricket brain on his shoulders. I'm pleased he built a good Test career from that trip. For long periods, he carried the England pace attack on his shoulders and he fought back bravely time after time from some terrible injuries. Not many bowlers of Bob's height manage to keep going for such a long time.

I felt very sorry, though, for Alan Ward. In my book, this lad had everything a fast bowler needs, except devil and fire in his belly. He was just too nice a bloke. When we arrived in Australia, the papers were full of Snow and Ward, England's deadly strike force – you could see Snowy visibly growing in stature with all the publicity while Alan got smal-

ler. He was too nice to summon up much hatred for the batsmen. Then he got injured and had to go home.

The Third Test at Melbourne was rained off without a
ball being bowled and then we were lumbered with an extra
Test at the request of the Australian Board. They needed the
money, because Melbourne over the New Year period brings
in huge crowds. We didn't really fancy an extra Test because
of the strain on our fast bowlers but we had no option – so
there were four Tests still to go.

We went one-up in the Fourth Test at Sydney with the
aid of some magnificent fast bowling from Snowy, two brilliant batting displays by Boycott and a solid all-round performance by everyone else. Again I got a fascinating insight into
Illingworth's captaincy. At the close of the second day, I told
Ray I fancied a bowl because I thought the conditions would
suit me. He'd ignored my hints in the last session of that day
and I thought no more of it. Well, Redpath was not out overnight and looking ominously solid; in the nets the next morning, the ball was swinging for me and Ray asked how I felt.
'Fine, I'm still swinging the ball, Ray', I replied and he smiled.
We all filed out at the start of the day and I wheeled off to my
accustomed position at third man. Ray called me over to open
the bowling! I spluttered, 'Are you kidding, man?' Snowy's got
to bowl from this end. Those blokes in the press box would
crucify you if you didn't.' He told me to get on with it; I got
Redpath with my second ball and Johnny Gleeson shortly
afterwards. Ray said, 'Right, off you go to third man'; he
brought back Snow and we finished with a lead of nearly a
hundred. Just imagine if Ray's hunch hadn't come off!

This was Graham McKenzie's last Test. For some years,
he was almost the entire Australian attack and eventually he
was bowled into the ground. A quiet, easy-going guy, he
would have been an even greater bowler if he'd had the devil
of a Lillee. With a beautiful action, he was deceptively fast – of
all the bowlers I've faced, he was the one who hit my bat the
hardest. But it amazes me how the Aussies go off their sporting heroes; McKenzie was five wickets short of his 250 in
Tests when the match began, and he was struggling to get
them. One of the cricket writers saw fit to pen the following
sentence in a Sydney paper – 'Why doesn't someone give

Graham McKenzie the necessary five wickets for his 250 and then tell him to get the hell out of the game?' What a way to assess a great, uncomplaining fast bowler!

I had words with Boycott in that Test. I'd heard about his habit of pinching the strike at the end of the over and this was the first time I'd experienced it. I bided my time for a few overs and then said, 'Boycs, if you want the strike all the time, then say so. But don't keep trying to steal it from me, because I'm not here just to run for you!' He was fine after that and we continued to get on very well. Sometimes he just needed a few well-chosen words.

The Aussies simply buckled in the last innings against some superb fast bowling by Snow. Only two men got in double figures and Lawry carried his bat for 60 out of 116. Lawry, a dogged, big-innings man who was a great runner between the wickets, never tried to take the strike as his side fell apart. He just stood his ground and picked up the odd run here and there while Snowy ripped through at the other end.

Lawry killed the Test stone dead by leaving us only four hours to get 270. As we had Brian Luckhurst nursing a broken finger and I had a badly bruised toe, it wasn't exactly a tempting declaration and we were quite happy to consolidate our lead in the series.

I scored a century in that Melbourne Test. When I walked to the wicket, we were 88 for 3 in reply to their total of 493. Brian Luckhurst was out there, and the crowd was making a terrible din as they knocked their beer cans together. It was simply a matter of playing out the day and trying to hold things together. At the end of the over, I joined Brian in the middle of the wicket and looked around at the baying crowd. 'Christ, Brian, I don't know about you, but I feel very lonely out here,' I said. 'So do I, Bas, let's keep meeting like this!' he said. Well, we put on over a hundred and at the end of the Saturday's play, I was not out 70-odd and well pleased. I'd come in at a bad time, stuck to my task and hadn't got out when I was tired near the end. Kerry O'Keeffe, their new leg-spinner, had bowled me a magnificent over. He beat me four times and rapped my pad; each time the crowd went up with a mighty roar, but I survived. That night, I was having a few self-satisfied beers when some guys came across to me and said, 'What about that over O'Keeffe bowled at you, then?' I said, 'That was a great over but don't forget – you open the paper tomorrow morning and see what I've scored.' That was typical of the Aussies – they give you nothing and you just have to stand up for yourself. They always want to drink more than you, to out-argue you, to get on top.

One other unsavoury incident in that Test was one of the first crowd invasions to celebrate a batsman's hundred that I can remember. This has become a regrettable fact of modern Test cricket but, in those days, it was still judged to be a heresy. This was a full-scale invasion. About 2,000 people swarmed over the ground when Ian Chappell got to his hundred; we sat down on the ground and some kid came up, told Colin Cowdrey he had no idea how to play the game and proceeded to pinch his white hat! A stump was also stolen. Somewhere in the world, an offensive young lad who, hopefully, has now grown up a little, may still be the proud possessor of Colin Cowdrey's sunhat. I wonder if he shows it off to his mates?

A slow, easy-paced Adelaide pitch meant Australia would really have to work for victory in the Sixth Test. As we led off with 470, there was little chance of that. That was the game where Ray was furious at Snowy and all the press boys who slated Ray for not enforcing the follow-on should know the story.

The Aussies were 235 behind on the first innings and normally the follow-on request would be automatic. But we were in the middle of an incredible sequence of Tests and our quickies were getting tired. As we came off the field, Ray asked me if we should make them follow-on. I said we should, even though the bowlers were shattered by the effort put into this innings and from the previous weeks. When we got into the dressing-room, the bowlers made it clear what they thought – they were already in the shower, looking forward to a nice, long rest. For the first time I could recall, Ray didn't back his own judgement, but sent out our openers for the second innings.

When we declared and set them an impossible total, we had eight and a half hours to bowl them out. Ray asked Snowy for a really big effort at the start to dislodge Lawry,

Stackpole and Ian Chappell. 'I want the quickest you can give for about five overs – and then you won't have to bowl any more after that,' he said. Snowy just loped in and turned his arm over and Ray got mad. He grabbed the ball off him after a few overs and said, 'Right, get off to third man.' Ray felt let down and I don't blame him; no captain of my experience looked after his fast bowlers better. He'd put them under wraps and under-bowl them. He'd get me and Underwood to hold things together till the fast men were refreshed – but woe betide the fast bowler if he didn't do his stuff when Ray asked for it. Perhaps Ray's anger had something to do with Snowy's superb bowling which won us the Final Test at Sydney.

That Sydney Test was the greatest match I ever played in. The tension throughout was unbelievable on every day. The Aussies had made some changes and Ian Chappell had replaced Lawry as skipper, a sensible choice because he was much more dynamic and a good man to lead from the front when nothing other than a victory will do. What pleased me most about that game was that everyone in the England side chipped in with a useful performance at some stage of the game – useful runs, an important wicket or a great catch. It was a classic team effort under a great captain, who never flapped for a moment. We were up against it right from the start because we'd lost Boycott with a broken arm, sustained a few days previously on the greenest Sydney wicket you could imagine. It was such a dangerous wicket that Graham McKenzie was bowling full tosses and slow half-volleys to make sure the ball didn't rear up. So we were without our star batsman and for most of the final Australian innings, we were without our star fast bowler, John Snow, who broke his bowling hand on the boundary fence, running for a catch. So we were really in the cart – and the Aussies only needed 223 to win.

At the close of the fourth day, the game was beautifully poised; they needed about 120 to win with five wickets left, including Greg Chappell and Walters. On the way back to the hotel, Ray said to me, 'Do you know, Bas, I'd give anything to win tomorrow, absolutely anything.' It was the first time I'd seen him show emotion and I realized then how much pressure he'd been taking over the past few months. So I thought I could confide in him; I told him I had a chance of

28 and **29** The contrasting world of a batsman – the cover drive (with the right hand doing all the work!) and then that sinking feeling we all know so well. The successful bowler was Warwickshire's Steve Rouse.

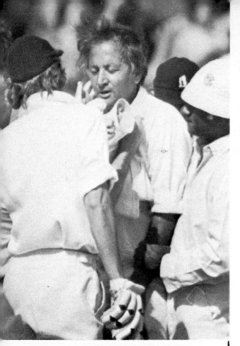

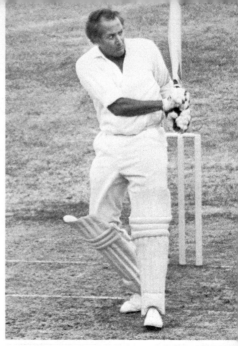

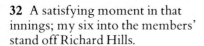

30 Glazed eyes and a sore cheekbone after being hit by Warwickshire's David Brown when I mistimed my hook shot.

31 The Benson and Hedges Final, 1976, when I batted on one leg against Kent.

32 A satisfying moment in that innings; my six into the members' stand off Richard Hills.

33 I'm getting near to my fifty and the strain is beginning to tell. But my partner, Gordon Wilcock, is on hand to encourage the old warrior.

34 For lovers of irony, a picture that will probably never be seen again in my lifetime – a coloured South African (myself), a white South African (Eddie Barlow) and a West Indian (Derryck Murray) playing in the same international match. The occasion was the Edgbaston Test of 1970 when the Rest of the World took over the series from the banned South Africa.

35 A relaxing moment in the Brisbane Test, 1970. At the back are John Snow and Colin Cowdrey, Keith Fletcher is on my left and Derek Underwood is on my far left.

36 My last Test, the Oval, 1972 – and Greg Chappell catches me off Ashley Mallett.

37 Pictured with my dear friend, 'Benny' Bansda, just before he died in 1973. He was the man who, above all, got me to England in 1960.

38 It's 1980 and the wheel has come full circle – I'm now the coach at Worcester and my old mate Roy Booth (now chairman of the cricket committee) talks me through my contract.

39 Naomi shows us how to do it. Eat your heart out Rachel Heyhoe Flint!

seeing the great Mexican singer, Jose Feliciano, at the Hilton that night. It was his last night and I thought that would help ease the tension I was feeling. I told Ray the show would probably finish by about half-past midnight and I'd be in bed shortly afterwards. He looked at me and said slowly, 'Put it this way, Bas. We're one day away from crowning a great tour for us. There are a lot of people from England in our hotel and they've come all this way and paid good money to see us play for our country. There are also a lot of people who didn't want me to bring you out on this trip because they said you were too old. But I wanted you with me and I'm glad I stuck by you because you've had a good trip. I know you won't do anything stupid tonight but what if some of our English supporters see you at the show tonight – and then tomorrow morning, someone whacks the ball up in the air and you drop it. You know what they'll say – that you were out boozing till two o'clock in the morning! But I'll leave it all up to you.'

He wasn't a bad psychologist, was he? I didn't go, I stayed in my room all night, watched TV yet didn't go to bed till one in the morning. The next morning, Walters went to cut Willis, got a thick edge and I took a swirler at third man. Ray came up to me and said, 'I told you it was a good idea to stay in last night!'

Ray needed all his coolness in the Aussie first innings when the crowd got really nasty after Snowy hit Jenner in the face with a bouncer. Snowy had a score to settle with Jenner because when we played South Australia, he was caught behind off Snowy – but he wasn't given out and he stood there laughing. I didn't think Snowy would forget that and as Jenner walked to the wicket at Sydney, I said to Keith Fletcher, 'He's got a helpful wicket here – I think we might see a few bouncers.' Sure enough he toppled Jenner when he bowled a vicious bouncer and the batsman turned his back and it hit him on the back of the head. Snowy said, 'Is he okay?' and then turned and walked back to his mark. That did it for the crowd – after all, Jenner was number ten batsman and they weren't to know that our man had asked if he was hurt, although not very ostentatiously.

Snow aggravated the situation by standing right against

the boundary rope when he wasn't bowling – and the crowd, within touching distance of the so-called villain, started baying at him. Someone threw a full can of beer on to the field, a drunk grabbed Snowy by the arm and Ray stormed off the field with his side. As we sat in the dressing-room Ray told our manager we weren't going back until the crowd were told to behave and that if it happened again, we would be off for the day. I think he was entitled to do this and such clear-headed action by the skipper only made us admire him even more. On that great morning, when we rolled over the Aussies, Ray bowled absolutely beautifully. He judged the angles perfectly, nagged away at the batsmen, preyed on their nerves and just psyched them out. At the end we carried him off the field and started on one of the best parties I can ever remember. It isn't every day England regain the Ashes on Australian soil – Ray was the first captain to do so since Jardine in 1932/3.

But before the big party started, I had the honour of meeting the great English fast bowler, Harold Larwood. He had emigrated to Australia twenty years previously but never came near the England tourists after an unfortunate incident on a previous tour. Colin Cowdrey – in a typically kind gesture – went to find Larwood and brought him to the triumphant English dressing-room. I was introduced to him and we talked about the Bodyline days when he terrorized the Aussie batsmen. He told me, 'Douglas Jardine, our skipper, told us to hate the Australians. But I set out to get them caught in the leg-trap, not to injure them. Bradman and I haven't been friends since.' At that moment our dressing-room door opened and in walked Sir Donald Bradman! He said, 'Congratulations, Basil' and to Larwood, 'Hello, Lol' and walked on. After all those years, they still harboured deep feelings about each other.

After a couple of days' celebration and hangover-cursing in Sydney, we flew to New Zealand to play two more Tests. I always feel sorry that those warm, hospitable people in New Zealand have to make do with an England team that's tired, homesick and feeling rather anti-climatic about playing them after the tensions of battling for the Ashes. It's softer and more pleasant than in Australia and so you tend to unwind rather too much and fail to do yourself justice on the field. I was pleased with my hundred, though, in the Test at Christchurch on a damp wicket with the ball keeping low. One shot I played in that knock still lingers in the memory; I played Vic Pollard so sweetly off my legs that it hit the fence and rebounded halfway back to the stumps. I didn't put any power at all in the shot, it was all timing. I wish they all looked like that.

So the tour was over. Even though I shouldn't have gone due to my age, I was happy with my overall contribution, despite those creaking bones round the boundary edge. It's a young man's tour, but Ray Illingworth nursed me through. There were many magnificent performers for England on that tour – the bowling of Snow, the batting of Edrich, Boycott and Luckhurst and the wicket-keeping of Knott. He was absolutely superb behind the stumps; he made just one error as far as I could see, when he missed an easy stumping of Marsh in the last Test. But at least that proved he was human. Knotty worked harder at his game than anyone I've ever known; he'd be out there practising every morning to keep supple. People think that it's just natural ability that gets him through but I maintain he worked twice as hard as any other cricketer I've seen.

Although John Snow grabbed most of the fast bowling headlines, I thought Peter Lever was magnificent. He only picked up 13 wickets in five Tests but time after time, he'd bowl uphill or into the wind so that Snowy could have the best conditions. Peter was one of the crucial components in Illingworth's 'hold it together' policy when there was no hope of getting a victory by a chance of being beaten. He didn't know how to give his team-mates less than a hundred per cent.

10 Final Test Appearances

After the Australian trip, I played eleven more times for England. That was more times than I expected but Ray was skipper and I think he felt I could still do my stuff. I fielded mostly in the slips or gully area in those final years and although I didn't miss all that many, my eyes weren't the same, especially when the snicks from the quickies were flying around. But Ray stuck with me. It was a tricky time for English cricket. Although we'd regained the Ashes, we weren't really a great side. The skipper just papered over the cracks and nursed us along. In the previous couple of years we had lost batsmen of the calibre of Cowdrey, Graveney, Milburn and Barrington. You don't replace men like those overnight and Ray had to make the most of what he'd got until the younger breed acquired experience.

He was doubly unfortunate in that the 1971 tourists were at last emerging from the status of being second-class Test countries. Both Pakistan and India had been pushovers for as long as I could remember but in 1971 it was a different proposition. The Pakistan batsmen were very impressive and they would have beaten us at Edgbaston but for rain and should have won at Leeds. India managed to win a series in England for the first time, thanks to some magnificent spin bowling, brilliant catching and shrewd captaincy.

The First Test against Pakistan was notable for an innings of 274 by a young man I'd never heard of: Zaheer Abbas. The Edgbaston wicket was a beauty and he absolutely slaughtered us. Yet he was very flashy outside the off-stump. Ray even bet Brian Luckhurst that Zaheer wouldn't make another fifty in the series because he'd used up all his luck in that great innings. Well he made 72 at Leeds and Brian won the bet but the off-stump area certainly seemed to be the place where he was most vulnerable. He's improved a lot since then; he's tightened up his game and scored runs all over the world, the sign of a great player.

The Pakistanis kept us in the field till the third morning

when they reached 600. It was the longest time I'd ever fielded – the old bones were aching, I can tell you. And I didn't have much time to rest them, either – I came in when we were 46–3, got a good 70-odd but we still had to follow-on. In the second knock, the rain saved us but not before I was given out. Asif Masood bowled me a bouncer, I hooked it just behind square and Mushtaq picked it up on the half-volley. I stood my ground and the umpire gave me out. That night, Asif maintained that the ball hadn't bounced. Two weeks later I played against Mushtaq in a county match and he said he thought the ball could have hit the ground before he caught it.

Rain ruined any chance of a clear-cut result at Lord's so it was off to Leeds where we won a magnificent match by 25 runs. Leeds again proved my lucky ground – I made a couple of seventies and in the second knock, I was dismissed by a quite brilliant catch by Wasim Bari behind the stumps – he had to change direction and take a low one in front of first slip. In this match he equalled the Test record with eight catches and he looked a very good keeper. It's funny how the good Test sides always have a fine keeper.

It was a cracking Test all the way through with the ball moving about and runs hard to come by. They needed 231 to win, the lowest total of the match, and at one stage they were 160 for 4. But the pressure got to them, just as Sadiq and Asif Iqbal were running away with the game. Norman Gifford went over the wicket to Asif, he had a rush of blood to the head, elected to charge down the wicket and Knott stumped him. Then Ray Illingworth played another one of his hunches, brought me on to bowl and I got Intikhab and Sadiq in the space of five deliveries. Old Golden Arm strikes again! I can still hear Sadiq's howl of disappointment as he hit a slow full toss straight back at me!

They fell apart then and we nicked it at the end. Once again, though, it was a triumph for Ray's captaincy. We really should have lost and at the start of the final day, with just about 200 needed and all their wickets in hand, not many would have backed us. Instead of starting off the attack conventionally with his two fast bowlers, Ray decided to bowl himself. He got Aftab Gul with the third ball of the day and had Zaheer caught next ball. The hunch had paid off yet again.

Ray's skill in tactical terms was again obvious in the next Test – at Lord's against the Indians. They only needed just over 180 to win at about forty an hour but he played on the batsmens' nerves throughout with imaginative field placing and tight, nagging bowling. The Indians started to fret with rain clouds gathering and an historic victory within their grasp. They lost wickets to reckless shots and when rain prevented any play after tea, they were 38 runs short with just two wickets in hand and England then were in the box seat.

But it had been gripping stuff all the way through. Scoring was slow throughout and some people who don't understand the true nature of Test cricket thought it was all very boring. But any match which contains as much high-class spin bowling, from players like Bedi, Venkat, Chandrasekhar, Gifford and Illingworth, surely can't be boring. I found it tense, exacting and hard work – just what a Test should be.

But that match will chiefly be remembered for the Snow/Gavaskar incident, when Snow barged the little Indian to the ground while he was attempting a sharp single off his bowling on that tense final day. Things hadn't gone very well for Snowy since coming back from Australia as the world's best fast bowler. Sussex had dropped him for a month because of his poor form and he was really having a hard time of it. Obviously England couldn't play him against the Pakistanis, as he was short of match practice, so this Lord's game was his first Test of the summer.

I was standing in the slips when the incident happened. Engineer tapped the ball, and went for a single with Gavaskar. I remember Snowy running up from the bowler's end, and looking for Gavaskar out of the corner of his eye; when he came level with the bowler, Snowy leant on him and sent him flying. Snowy then threw him his bat and the game went on. There was a big uproar about the incident and I said to Snowy in the dressing-room, 'What the hell did you do that for?' He said that Gavaskar got in his way, but then Ray told us both to shut up. Just then, the action replay of the incident was shown on the dressing-room TV. They stopped the action just as Snowy drew level with Gavaskar and it was clear he was waiting for the little Indian. Snowy, realizing that he'd been well and truly caught out, said, 'Well, the

scene's been far too quiet without me, anyway.' He knew he
was out of order, he was made to apologize to the Indians, and
was rightly dropped for one Test.

Just by way of a change, rain ruined the next Test at Old
Trafford and we came to the Oval all-square. We were hustled
out for 101 in the second innings and they got the necessary
173, to win by four wickets. It was our first defeat in 26 official Tests (if you don't count the Rest of the World series) and
that was a tribute to Illingworth's skills as a captain. Indeed,
on that last day, when the Indians had plenty of time to get the
runs, he bowled absolutely beautifully. In 36 overs, he gave
away just 40 runs and if Derek Underwood had bowled anywhere near as well as the skipper, we would have won. At that
time, Derek was bowling far too quickly; Norman Gifford
kept him out for most of the summer because Ray felt that
Gifford was a better bowler on good wickets, with his extra
flight. I think he was right. Derek became a great bowler but it
was Ray who made him think about his bowling by leaving
him out.

We lost that Test because of some superb leg-spin bowling by Chandrasekhar. We had a lead of 70-odd on the first
innings but we had no answer to Chandra's fast leg-spin on a
slow Oval pitch. He got more out of that wicket than anybody else and his close fielders supported him superbly by
turning half-chances into catches. No one could begrudge the
Indians their victory – they were a lovely team to play against,
they never complained, they got on with the game and had a
pleasant word for everybody on the field. Their slow bowlers
were a delight to play against, in an era dominated by seamers.
As my top score in six innings against them was just 30, I
think it's fair to say they had the better of that contest.

So to my last Test series, and a good one. I always loved
playing against the Aussies and this 1972 series was a good
tight one with an interesting contrast between the sides. We
were, to say the least, a fairly venerable outfit with old hands
like Peter Parfitt, Mike Smith, John Price, Ray Illingworth and
myself involved, while the Aussies, as usual, put their trust in
youngsters under the aggressive captaincy of Ian Chappell.
Although the series was squared two-all with England retain-
ing the Ashes, the Aussies came out of it with greater plusses –

a fine batsman/wicket-keeper in Marsh, a great fast bowler in Lillee, solid batsmen like Edwards, Stackpole and the Chappells and some brilliant fielders. The foundations of that hard, mean, brilliantly successful Australian side of the mid-seventies were laid in that 1972 series.

But England under Illingworth would never miss an opportunity to strike and we did so in the First Test at Old Trafford in typically English conditions. The ball moved all over the place for the first four days and Snow, Arnold and Greig prospered in conditions they were used to. On a cloudy day, with the ball moving about, I'd always back England because we've got more experience of the conditions. Dennis Lillee showed his lack of experience in the first innings; he bowled much too short when he should have bowled a slower, fuller length. But Ray Lindwall had a word with him and in the second knock, he bowled magnificently, taking six wickets, including D'Oliveira with a superb outswinger. In the end, Rod Marsh could have won the game for Australia; he played a great knock for 91 while the others threw their wickets away in conditions that were now ideal for batting – but just when we were getting worried, Marsh played a rash shot and was caught by Knott. So we went one up but we'd seen enough to know that things wouldn't always be so comparatively easy.

The next Test at Lord's will always be known as 'Massie's Match', and rightly so. Sixteen wickets on your Test debut! I've never seen a man swing a ball so much – thank God he didn't play at Old Trafford! He did it against some English batsmen who'd been around a bit yet none of us could master him – poor Mike Smith suffered the ignominy of being bowled round his legs! It was a difficult match to umpire because the ball was swinging around so much and I reckon that if 'Dickie' Bird had been umpiring at Lord's there wouldn't have been one LBW – with him, you've got to be right back on your stumps to be out LBW when the ball's moving about. But I don't want to take anything away from Massie; in the English dressing-room, we were glued to the TV trying to spot how Massie managed to swing it so much – and we found out too late. We finally spotted a sign that told us when he was going to bowl the outswinger – his arm would make a complete circle – yet when he bowled the inswinger, his arm would only come from his chin. So he would pull himself back further for the outswinger and put in less effort for the inswinger. He never varied his angle of delivery, his footmarks were always in the same place so the alteration of swing just had to come from his arm. But by the time the assembled brains of English cricket had worked that out, we'd lost by eight wickets!

It was rumoured that Massie was using grease to swing the ball – for how else could it be boomeranging about after sixty overs? Ray tested this idea at the Leeds Test a month later. Ray rubbed grease on one side of the ball and asked me to slip it in on occasions when I was bowling in the nets. Peter Parfitt was the unlucky batsman and he finally gave up against a ball that swung all over the place. He was getting bowled so much by this ball that he stopped batting, in case his confidence suffered! But as Massie's influence was already starting to decline, Ray didn't pursue things.

I'm often asked why Massie declined so spectacularly. Well, he wouldn't often get conditions so suitable to his style of bowling, certainly not abroad. He didn't have much variety, unlike Lillee, and once we'd sorted out how to spot the out-swinger, we played him well enough for the remaining Tests, when he picked up just seven more wickets. But nobody can ever take away the glory from Bob Massie of an amazing display of swing bowling.

The Third Test at Trent Bridge ended up as a bore. They set us over 400 to win on a flat wicket but we lost a quick wicket and never gave it a go. Tony Greig and I had to play through the last afternoon, thinking purely of survival. It was boring for us, for the fielders and most of all, for the spectators. I hope people realize it's no fun at all to sit on the splice and just endure for a few hours but Ian Chappell gave us simply no option. And to be fair to Greigy and myself, we weren't exactly slow-coaches most of the time.

Things were a lot more dramatic in the Fourth Test at Leeds. The Aussies were rolled over in just two and a half days and they complained that the wicket had been doctored for Underwood, who took ten wickets in the match. The truth is that the groundsman couldn't do a thing about the terrible weather of the previous week which left the pitch slightly suspect – but Test Match players should show more resolution on a wearing wicket than Chappell's lot did. Only Stackpole and Sheahan showed much stomach for the fight while Illingworth and Snow, in a vital stand of over a hundred, demonstrated what could be done with resolution and a little luck. If the wicket was so bad, it would obviously favour the side batting first, yet the Aussies won the toss and threw away that priceless advantage. If they'd left us to get about 200 in the last innings, they surely would have caused us trouble. But they only had one authentic spinner, Mallett, and their side wasn't properly balanced. At lunch on the first day, they were 70–1, yet they tumbled to 146 all out. If things were all right before lunch, how could they blame the pitch for such bad batting in the hour afterwards? Underwood is unplayable on a wicket that helps him a lot but I don't think that Leeds track was all that bad. A good English county side with some solid, sensible batting would have fared much better. Playing Test cricket in England is so vital for an overseas batsman's education.

Things were nicely set up for the final Test at the Oval. It was to be played to a finish and we lost by five wickets because we bowled badly on a wicket that was starting to turn. Marsh and Sheahan steadied them when half the side were out and they were still 70-odd short but we were hampered by an ankle injury to Ray, and Derek Underwood again failed to slow things down; he was still pushing it through too quickly and not getting much turn. It would have been interesting to see how my own county captain, Norman Gifford, might have fared on that wicket where flight and turn were essential to bowl a side out.

All credit, though, to the Aussies – the Chappell brothers both hit fine centuries, Lillee took ten wickets in the match and their side was maturing rapidly. Two years previously, Marsh looked the worst keeper I'd ever seen in Test cricket – now the change in him was amazing. He'd lost a lot of weight, his footwork was much better and his hands were very much safer. Lillee had learned a lot since Old Trafford; his control was masterly, his variation subtle and he was really quick when he wanted to be. Their fielding was athletic and clean – with Ross Edwards and Paul Sheahan each dominating one side of the wicket, so that sometimes they seemed to have twelve men. And Ian Chappell was a hard, remorseless captain who seemed to play even better under the responsibilities of leadership.

It was my last Test and unfortunately I couldn't repeat the glories of my previous Oval Test against the Aussies. The Chappell brothers caught me out twice – Greg at short leg off Mallett and finally Ian in the slips from a Massie outswinger. As I walked off in the second innings, I knew that was the end of it for me with England. We were due to tour India that winter but I knew I wouldn't be picked, I was too old. I could still bat but fielding was now my downfall. By now the press was full of the 'Dad's Army' jibe; they wanted to see fresh faces, even though it is performances that surely count, not a player's age. Nevertheless, it was time for a clear-out and as I always knew the selectors took notice of the press, I realized I would be among the first to go. I was perfectly philosophical, though; I'd toured three times with England, scored hundreds for them at home and abroad and apart from that disastrous West Indian tour, hadn't let them down. Everything was a plus for me after Lord's 1966. It was now high time to devote myself to my county.

11 Playing for Worcester

I can't think of any cricketer who doesn't like playing at New Road, Worcester. With due respect to other county grounds, you'd have to be a little blasé not to feel rather special as you walk out on to that immaculate playing surface, check that the Cathedral is looking its usual elegant self and let the eye wander around the scene; not too many office blocks in sight, but plenty of trees. The River Severn is a six-hit away and there are friendly faces everywhere. Players from other counties often remark to me that everyone seems so cheerful at Worcester – the club officials, the spectators, the evening paper sellers. I tell them, 'Wouldn't you be cheerful if you played or watched cricket here?'

Lancashire was my instinctive choice back in 1963 but that was more to do with gratitude to the good folk of Middleton and my inhibitions about building a career and a new life for myself and family in strange surroundings. I needn't have worried; I've been treated excellently by the committee at Worcester and the atmosphere is something special. Although I retired in 1979, I still spend a lot of time at my beloved New Road, even when I'm not coaching. In the winter, I'll play football on the boundary edge with my two sons, and at night I can be seen running round the ground for an hour – now that surprises those of you who thought I just turned up and played, doesn't it? New Road still means so much to me. My home is a mile away and I used to love strolling home on a golden summer's day after playing well and having a few pints with my friends in the clubhouse.

I've been lucky to be part of a fine side since I joined the county in 1964. In that period, we won the county championship three times, the John Player League once and appeared in three Cup Finals at Lord's, losing the lot. Not many counties can match that record over a 15-year span. We were lucky enough to have about four match-winners in our team over the years, so that if conditions weren't favourable and we were up against it, a Graveney, a Gifford, a Turner or a Flavell would pull something out of the bag, with loyal, unsung help from the others. We've always been a professionally-minded side with a good collective temperament. We showed that many times – not least in 1965 when we won the last nine games on the trot to snatch the title and again in 1974 when a fine late run plus favourable weather helped whisk the championship from under Hampshire's nose.

So many critics called us lucky when we won the 1974 title and to a certain extent we were. But we played magnificent cricket in that final month and we got the crucial bowling points by excellent play. Hampshire were due to play Yorkshire at Bournemouth and we were at Chelmsford playing Essex. Luck went our way with the toss, we put Essex in on a drying wicket. Gifford took 7–15 and we got the full bonus points, which put us ahead of Hampshire by just two points. If we'd lost the toss, I'm sure they would have put us in and we wouldn't have gathered so many batting points before the rain came down. Anyway it rained all weekend but at least we'd squeezed in some play. Over at Bournemouth, it was washed out without a ball being bowled. At lunch on the final day, our game was called off and we'd just sneaked home.

Great was the sorrow in Hampshire but I must point out that although they made the running throughout the summer, we won an extra game – eleven compared to ten. We both drew six and lost three, so the crucial factor was that extra victory. Over a season, isn't it fair that the title should go to the side that wins more games?

I wish I could understand how we never win our Cup Finals at Lord's. We've played in two Gillette Finals (1963 and 1966) and two Benson and Hedges Finals (1973 and 1976) and didn't win any of them. Poor old Norman Gifford played in all four matches – unlucky for him! We all loved playing there, the atmosphere is tremendous on Final day, and we had enough players with big-match temperament to prosper in such an atmosphere – but we never made it.

I played in three of the Finals – in 1966 we lost by five wickets to our near-neighbours, Warwickshire. I was annoyed at myself for getting out to a wild stroke off David Brown and when I got back to the dressing-room, Jack Flavell had a go at me. I shouted, 'Don't you tell me how to play the game' – one

of those marvellously tolerant remarks we cricketers come out
with on occasions of stress! Jack was quite right, though, there
was a lot of responsibility on my shoulders and I failed because
of rashness. In 1973 I think our tactics let us down against
Kent; we needed 220–odd to win and I was pushed down the
order while a left-hander, Rodney Cass, was sent in to try to
counteract Derek Underwood, who doesn't normally like
bowling against left-handers. But Rodney had already kept
wicket in that game and it was too much to expect him to bat
like a number four. Norman Gifford came in at number six to
try to get after Underwood with some rustic left-hander's
blows but that failed and I ended up coming in at number
seven with too much to do. I managed forty-odd but they
won by 39 runs. It was worth a gamble, I suppose, but on
reflection, Cup Final day is the time for the blokes who are
used to batting at four or five.

The 1976 Benson and Hedges Final was also against Kent
and again we lost it but not before I played an innings which
still gives me immense satisfaction. I tore a hamstring while
fielding; it was absolute agony and I knew I couldn't possibly
bat. I couldn't walk up the stairs, our physio had to drag me
up and he packed the leg in ice. I thought I might be able to
stand with a bat in my hand but the medical experts said, 'not
a chance, it's a bad one'. Norman Gifford pleaded with them,
but it seemed hopeless. Then the game started slipping away
from us when we batted and Giffie said, 'Can't you help, Bas?'
The doctor suggested strapping up the whole of my leg so that
I would have no feeling at all, not even in my toes. So I gave it
a try and hobbled out to bat. I was thinking about my
strategy: I decided to get as far over to the off-stump as I could
and then give it a slog on the leg-side. I wanted to hit Derek
Underwood over extra cover's head if I could, so I just stood
there and carved. My left leg was giving me agony and I could
only play off my back foot; I dreaded getting a bouncer
because I wouldn't have had a hope of avoiding it. I took middle and off guard so that I didn't have to worry too much
about footwork; if I missed a straight one, I was out, simple as
that. I kept my left foot slightly off the ground and hit
through the line of the ball whenever it came near me. My
power and the fact that I was a back-foot player obviously

helped me. My best shot was a six over mid-off from the seam bowling of Richard Hills. Eventually, at 50, I chanced my arm once too often and I was bowled off my pads, hitting across the line.

I was overwhelmed by the reception I got as I walked in. I kept my head down, in case I got too embarrassed. My pride received an even greater boost when the player who deservedly won the 'Man of the Match' award came in to see me. Graham Johnson had made a beautiful 78 and taken four fine catches in the deep, a worthy winner in my book. But he came to me and said, 'I wish I could give you this.' A nice gesture from a sportsman and much appreciated.

I enjoyed the day we won the John Player League in 1971. We had to score 126 within 17.5 overs to top Essex's run-rate of 4.519 an over. We did it with two balls to spare and finished with a run-rate of 4.522! We had to sweat for another week until Lancashire lost to Glamorgan – and then the trophy was ours by the barest of margins. What made our victory doubly sweet was that we beat Warwickshire in the final match. The game was at Dudley, where we've always enjoyed tremendous support. There were 10,000 people in the ground that day and they saw a magnificent innings from Ron Headley – he and Alan Ormrod put on 55 in 30 balls to win the match for us.

The title was a triumph for Norman Gifford, who missed the match through injury. This was his first season as captain and he subsequently improved all the time. In those early seasons he was a little dour in his leadership. A hard, professional cricketer, he was brought up in a hard school in the days when Worcestershire would never give a thing away and it showed at the start of his captaincy. But he's developed a lot since then and he'll go out and play cricket with anybody now. I don't think he's been far from the England captaincy on occasions – and he would be worth his place in the team.

I only captained Worcestershire once. It was in that 1971 season in Gifford's absence. We played at Edgbaston and after rain washed out the first day, I decided to make a game of it. Fortunately, Warwickshire's captain, Mike Smith, thought the same and in a game of three declarations, they scored 228 to win in $2\frac{1}{2}$ hours to climax a great two days' play. Kanhai and Jameson smashed us all over the place – I can still see Jameson hitting Bob Carter many a mile in his first over. But they were two terrific players and when they felt like it, any attack in the world would suffer. As we came off the field, Mike Smith said to me, 'Bas, when things like this go wrong, you look an absolute twit. I've just lost a game against Lancashire after I declared and I got some stick. But you went out there and played a game of cricket with us, so don't let them get at you.' Some of the members waited for me to complain about my declaration but I stand firm by my decision. It also put me off captaincy for good. Although I'd captained many sides in South Africa, the game was totally different over here. Although I was a great concentrator as a batsman and spectator, I'd occasionally doze off in the field. I'd sometimes lose interest while fielding and that wouldn't have been a good idea when skipper!

At least my Edgbaston decision had something to do with a great game of cricket immediately afterwards. We drove down to Chelmsford to play Essex, a team that would always try to play the game in the right spirit. Much of the credit for that went to Brian Taylor, their skipper, a man of strict principles about discipline but a captain who would always try for a win. Before the game started he came into our dressing-room and asked who led our side at Edgbaston. He turned to me and said, 'It's nice to know that Worcester's playing cricket again' – a reference to our recent past, when we tended to shut up shop and deny the opposition any room for manoeuvre. Well, Brian declared at lunchtime on the last day when he could easily have delayed it for another half-hour. He left us to get 250-odd in about three and a half hours . . . and we got them with an over to go. At the end he came to us and said, 'Well played, Worcester, now don't forget . . .' That's the way cricket should be played in my opinion. But that's also why, for instance, Gary Sobers wasn't all that effective as captain of Nottinghamshire. He would always try for a win and wouldn't simply play out time.

We had some marvellous times at Worcester during that championship-winning season of 1974. One match I'll never forget was the Yorkshire game at Hull – not simply because I scored 227, the highest of my first-class career. That was very satisfying, not least of all for a shot I played against the new ball. 'Rocker' Robinson pitched one short, it got up just below chest height and I flicked it. Somehow the timing was just right and it flew off the bat just behind square leg for six. David Constant, who was umpiring said to me, 'I can't make up my mind whether that was a good shot or you've got a bloody good bat in your hand!' But the really funny thing about that innings was a remark from Richard Hutton, that very amusing man. Richard always had me in stitches because of his dry wit – he was the man who once interrupted a monologue by Fred Trueman on his own exploits with the new ball with the words, 'Tell me Fred, would you say you were a modest man?' Collapse of great fast bowler! Anyway, Richard bowled a magnificent over in this Hull match against a lad who had stacks of ability but never really applied himself. His name was Ivan Johnson. He came from the Bahamas and he wasn't exactly black, more coffee-coloured, if you know what I mean. Everything was a laugh to Ivan, he never took offence at anything people said to him. Throughout this over, Richard Hutton was telling him he couldn't play, that he wasn't good enough to get a touch to the ball, etc, etc. I kept looking sideways, because if I'd looked at Richard I would have burst out laughing and I could tell he wasn't amused by Ivan's playing and missing and good-natured grinning. Finally Richard could stand it no longer; he bellowed down the wicket, 'Not only can't you play cricket – but I think it's about time you got back on your jam jar!'

More laughs came later in that match – courtesy of Jimmy Cumbes. Now Jim, as nice a bloke as anyone I know, was always known as 'Basil Baiter' in our dressing-room because he knew how to get me mad by pulling my leg in a subtle fashion. We were sitting in the dressing-room and Jim said, 'Hey lads, did you see the *Birmingham Post* this morning? They've taken a poll of their readers and Tony Greig's been elected the world's best all-rounder.' I wasn't thinking that Jim was having a go at me, so I carried on undressing and made for the showers, still turning the words over in my mind. It suddenly dawned on me that Jim couldn't have seen that day's edition of the *Birmingham Post* in Hull and I thought, 'He's having a go at me because Greigy's a white South African!' So I walked into the room again, said, 'Jimmy . . .' and they all burst out laughing.

Realizing I'd been set up, I said, 'Just you wait till tomorrow – we'll see who's the better all-rounder!' As luck would have it, we were playing Sussex in a Gillette Cup match, so I vowed to set my stall out. I got as good a hundred as I could wish and I managed to slog Greigy for a few as well. When he came in to bat, I said to the skipper, 'Give me that ball, Giffie, I'll get him out' – and I did, LBW for two! I said to Jim Cumbes, 'Now who's the best all-rounder?' and he loved it.

By the late 'seventies, my thoughts were turning to retirement. I was finding it hard going in the field, not when the ball came straight to me or when I had to throw but when I had to bend or turn sideways. I talked things over with the committee and they kept telling me to stay on for just one more season. I needed very little persuasion, I must admit, but I was worried about holding back promising young players like Dipak Patel and Cedric Boyns, who should really have been in the first team on a regular basis. But every time I was talked out of retirement I seemed to play better – in 1977, I topped the Worcestershire batting averages and in 1978, after my hundred against Lancashire, a local headmaster wrote to me and said he would always watch me provided I could still play an innings like that. I was genuinely flattered and I kept on playing. But the physical strain of playing seven-day-a-week cricket is great, when you get to my age – it's the only game I know where you *face* one way and *play* the other way, so that when you bat, the strain on the shoulders, ankles and knees eventually takes its toll. I still kept myself reasonably fit with my running but the danger period for me was always January or February, when I really had to force myself to get out into the cold and do my running. I still do about four miles a night, three nights a week, because I feel it's important to keep in trim. Who knows, my old county might face an injury crisis at some stage and have need of a venerable middle-order batsman?

I finally decided to call it a day at the start of the 1979 season. I didn't want to announce it officially because I dreaded all the fuss involved. My last county match was against Sussex on that lovely Worcester ground. I went out of county cricket in typically bizarre circumstances – I smashed a short ball from the off-spinner, Barclay, and it hit Graves just above the knee at silly point. From there it lobbed straight back to the bowler. Well, if you've got to go, do it in style!

Reality dawned when I walked out to bat in a John Player match at Edgbaston that season. Clear as a bell, I heard the youngster's voice shout, 'Where's your white stick?' I laughed to myself at his cheek but deep down, I thought, 'God, I don't want to go through too much of that.' I knew I could still bat – I proved that with a fifty I got against Somerset's Joel Garner when their keeper Derek Taylor told me that nobody had played him as well so far that season. That was a nice thing to say and I treasure it. But it was time to go before too many people started nudging each other and talking about the days when I wasn't such a bad player.

At the end of the season, I received an overwhelming tribute from the club. They invited all my past captains, the former capped players, the past presidents, the vice-presidents and the committee to a farewell dinner in my honour. I was presented with some beautiful cut glass that is now Naomi's pride and joy. The whole thing was too much for me – especially as the guest speaker was John Arlott. It was his first public speech for nine years and he missed the chance of a reception at 10 Downing Street for the Australia-bound England team. When it came to my turn to speak everything bubbled to the surface and I couldn't say all the things I wanted to say. Literally words failed me in my efforts to thank that marvellous club for all they'd done for me.

12 The Players

As I sat spellbound by John Arlott's oratory at the reception in my honour, my thoughts kept switching back and forth to my career in England. Len Coldwell's words in 1965 came back to me. 'What more can you hope for?' he had asked at the end of that first, championship-winning season. What more, indeed – certainly not an England cap.

I sat thinking about all the players I'd known and liked over the years. The characters like Eddie Barlow, John Snow, Fred Trueman and Wes Hall, the worriers like Geoff Boycott and Ken Barrington, the solid, uncomplaining triers like Peter Lever and David Brown, the unlucky ones like Colin Milburn, the 'shooting stars' like Bob Massie and the decent men like Colin Cowdrey, Graham McKenzie and Conrad Hunte. And the only cricketing genius I'd known, Gary Sobers.

Sobers was the greatest all-round cricketer of my generation. No bowler ever gave me more trouble consistently; for a few overs he was as quick as anybody I've faced, with a wicked, late in-ducker to the right-hand batsman. As a slow bowler he had a beautifully disguised slower delivery and as a fielder he was lithe and quick, with a great pair of hands anywhere. As a batsman, he was the best player I saw abroad. No one hit the ball harder and I used to dread fielding in the slips to Gary because he followed the correct doctrine that if you are going to flash at the ball, flash hard. You could never stand too far away in the slips for my liking when Gary batted.

It would be wrong to say the West Indies were a one-man team under Gary but when he went well, so did they, and when he struggled, the side struggled. He had an astonishing confidence in himself that was justly borne out by events. One West Indian player once said to me, 'The trouble with Gary is that, despite his genius, he thinks he's God on the field, that nothing can go wrong.' Years after his controversial declaration at Port of Spain that gave us the series in 1968 he was still being pilloried in the Caribbean. But Gary thought he could put things right on the field when we batted and he was also fed up with our time-wasting tactics. On neither count could I fault him. No cricketer of my time was better at putting things right on the field.

For me, Tom Graveney was the greatest all-round batsman of my time. By 'all-round' I mean on all wickets. He was simply a master; at Cheltenham he played an astonishing innings against two fine off-spinners, David Allen and John Mortimore. The wicket was simply turning square and I stood at the other end, watching a brilliant display of batting against these two England spinners. Quite simply, he 'charged' them; not one ball passed his bat on a wicket where the ball was jumping, as well as turning. If he missed the ball after jumping out to hit it, he made sure his pads or his body would stop it before the keeper moved in for the stumping. And his placement of shots on the on-side was out of this world.

Tom had such an impeccable technique, such a terrific temperament, that he could have gone on batting for another four years at least in first-class cricket. Even in his last season, he was the top Englishman with an average of 62. That sort of class was a rarity and I was privileged to see it at first hand. A lot of people told me that when younger he used to give it away against the quick bowlers. All I can say is that he played Wes Hall and co. so well at the age of forty that he must have been pretty special against the fast bowlers in earlier years. He was the only batsman I've seen who played them on the bounce off the front foot; that takes timing, bravery, coolness and high skill. I've seen him pull Hall and Griffith through mid-wicket, making them look like trundlers.

Apart from Boycott, I've never seen a man practice his batting more than Tom. If he was playing against a school eleven on a Sunday morning or a knock-up match in the West Indies, Tom would still have a net before the game started. He taught me a lot about attitude, as well. He used to say, 'There's no point in getting bothered about a bad run with the bat. Tomorrow's another day and if you're a good enough player, at the end of the season it will average itself out.' He always thought a few beers in the evening were preferable to moping in your room. Tom never altered socially, he was the same to everyone whether he'd got nought or a hundred and he taught me so much about the need for a balanced outlook on life. He was the man who stood beside me in the darkest moment of my life – when I heard I wasn't going to South Africa – and we will remain close for the rest of our lives.

I'm often asked about Geoff Boycott. What's he really like, they say? Well, my answer to that is 'I don't honestly know.' I speak as I find and I like him. I also admire him for the way he's kept bouncing back after he's been written off; I respect him for his dedication and I don't think his attitude to everyone is at all nasty. It's just that Geoff has always been wrapped up in the game that is basically his life and people keep sniping at him for that. He wasn't a great captain because he was so involved in his own performances that he couldn't really get to grips with the problems and morale of the other lads in the Yorkshire side – but there's no shame in that. Tom Graveney would have made a better captain if he'd thought less about his own batting. I always got on very well indeed with Boycs even though we were exact opposites in lifestyle. Perhaps he sensed that he wasn't the only one to have come up the hard way.

It was fascinating to play under three England captains of such contrasting styles. Colin Cowdrey preferred the waiting game while Ray Illingworth and Brian Close would try to make things happen once the opening was there. Of the three, Closey was the most attacking; his personal example at the Oval in 1966 was a fascinating instance of how a change of captain can help pick up a demoralized side. He didn't have a very good match with bat or ball but all the time we were aware of this bulldog of a man just dying to get at the West Indians. He would go through a brick wall to force a result; Closey didn't know how to defend, that's why he never really came to terms with the Sunday League slog involving fielders all round the boundary. His style of captaincy featured eight men round the bat, even though the scoreboard read 300 for 2!

Colin Cowdrey was a very gentle man with a deep love of the game and a very intellectual grasp of its tactics. A great theorist, Colin, he'd love to talk for hours about the niceties of cricket, even though for many of us it's really a simple game. I think sometimes he should have gone on to the attack more, instead of playing the waiting game. Perhaps the theories kept getting in the way. Nevertheless, he was a calm, composed captain who always treated me well and sympathetically.

But Ray Illingworth was the best skipper I've known; he had a knack of sensing things, of switching from defence to attack at just the right moment. He would use the technique of a Cowdrey and a Close at various stages but what set him apart was knowing that moment when to apply the pressure. Ray Illingworth got that right more times than most. He demanded everything from his players and, as John Snow can confirm, woe betide you if you didn't give him that commitment. But he'd still stand up for you in public even though he told you privately that you were wrong or you'd failed him in some way. No skipper got more out of his side than Ray.

The best slow bowler I've played against on English wickets would be Derek Underwood because of his ability to finish off a side when the wicket was helping him. But his influence abroad was limited, so for me, Bishen Bedi was the best on all wickets. A great bowler – control, flight, he had the lot. As he ran up to bowl I could sense him looking at me over his shoulder and saying, 'Do whatever you want to do, but I'll change direction and get you.' A lovely, placid guy, who played cricket as if he hadn't a care in the world. I remember when the Indians came to Worcester in 1974; Bishen was bowling as if the ball was on the end of a piece of string. The length and direction looked the same, only it wasn't. John Parker came down the wicket to him a couple of times and Bishen smiled to me at his end and said, 'It's only a matter of time, Basil!' It was – next over , he had John stumped from halfway down the pitch!

The best keeper of my time has been Alan Knott. His work on the 1970/71 tour of Australia was near perfection. I'd never seen wicket-keeping carried out at such a consistently high level. Poor Rod Marsh must have felt quite inadequate! Incidentally, has any touring side ever had two such brilliant keepers as Knotty and Bob Taylor? Both of them lovely lads, great company, never a word out of place and tremendously professional at their jobs. But Knotty shades it for me.

The best fast bowler? My dear old mate, Wes Hall. He was an awesome sight as he came in off that long run, with his feet stuttering halfway to tell you it was really going to be a quick one. The only way to play Wes was to take the fight to him – and then you had to look lively. But if you just tried to see him off, his strength was so great that he would just go on and on because he sensed you were struggling. He had a wonderful bowling action, and despite his aggression on the field, he was a true sportsman.

But so far, I've only talked about the great players. Every generation, however, throws up cricketers who become the 'nearly men' – those who had all the necessary qualities but for some reason, stayed on the fringe of Test status. These are the players who don't grab many newspaper headlines but keep doing a great job for their sides and earn the respect of their fellow-professionals. Here are a few names from my era that you might like to ponder.

Alan Jones: A remarkably consistent opening batsman for Glamorgan over the years. He was a nudger and deflector most of the time, but he could hit the ball hard when he wanted. He was one of those batsmen who just ticks over quietly – and the bowler gets a shock when he looks at the scoreboard and sees, 'Jones 50'. I think he missed out on England honours because Ray Illingworth didn't rate him in the field. He played in one match in 1970 against the Rest of the World and Ray didn't think he got a hundred per cent effort from him.

Brian Brain: I played with him for several years at Worcester and I rated him highly; in the same mould as Geoff Arnold and Peter Lever, he could run the ball away from the right-hander. He should have played for England but he was overshadowed a little at Worcester by Flavell and Coldwell and didn't get a kick up the backside when he deserved one. Sometimes he lacked a little commitment, as if he felt it was really a batsman's game. But I was very glad Brian made good because the best thing he ever did was to move to Gloucestershire after getting the sack at Worcester. Mike Procter took him in hand from the start and he and Brain became the best pair of opening bowlers in the country for a couple of seasons.

Don Shepherd: He bowled consistently well for Glamorgan, season in and season out. Predominantly a cutter, he bowled flat and sharply and was backed up by some marvellous close fielders. I suppose the flat Test wickets might not have suited his style of bowling – especially overseas – but he would regularly deliver the goods against England batsmen, so who's to say he wouldn't have made the grade at Test level?

Alan Ormrod: I don't care if you think I'm biased but I believe he's played the new ball as well as anyone in England in the last few seasons. He was in the shadows of Kenyon, Graveney and Turner for many seasons but he kept working at his game, sorting out the flashy shots from the safe ones and he plays quick bowling especially well. He doesn't hook or pull, he just moves out of the way or ducks. Some people were tipping him for England when he was about 17 which was silly, but I do think he might have got at least one cap. His technique is so sound that he should play for Worcestershire until he's at least forty.

Geoff Cook: Another of the sound opening batsmen that don't get the credit they deserve. Wayne Larkins, his opening partner, gets more attention because he's a stroke-player – but Cook plays the new ball better and in my opinion is superior to both Willey and Larkins as an all-round, correct player. A grafter with a fine, calm temperament, he doesn't bother with helmets – he just gets out of the way. If he doesn't play for England, I give up.

Ray East: A fine slow left-arm bowler, rather in the shade of Edmonds, Gifford and Underwood. He spins the ball a lot and would perform well abroad. Perhaps the cricket intelligentsia have been put off him because he clowns about a lot on the field. I agree he should be a little bit more disciplined while he's playing the game but it would be wrong to dismiss him for his frivolity.

Graham Johnson: An elegant, calm batsman who's suffered by being shunted up and down the Kent batting order. He's batted from one to seven for Kent and this, plus the development of his off-spinners, has retarded his progress towards becoming a top-class batsman. Very straight and correct, he has all the shots. A lovely fielder, I've never seen him look anything but class.

Robin Jackman: A bowler who'll try all day for you. Playing at the Oval isn't exactly guaranteed to send an opening bowler into raptures but Jackman has battled away for Surrey and done a marvellous job for them. Very aggressive and a useful batsman, he must have come very close to a tour for England, where his enthusiasm and all-round abilities might have taken him on to greater things. His lack of height didn't exactly help his bowling, but he could often make the ball rear up pretty steeply.

Pat Pocock: One of the finest spinners I've ever played against, he should have played more times for England – he seemed to lose his way after a great tour of the West Indies at the age of 21, when Kanhai, Sobers and the others never managed to collar him. I believe he tried to do too much with the ball, he was certainly always trying something different. He has come back strongly in recent years and I wouldn't be at all surprised if he at last realizes his potential. A beautiful action, a great theorist, he bowls a superb 'loop' ball.

Roger Prideaux: I always rated Roger highly. He really had to be dug out; so correct and strong when he batted, I wondered how the hell I was ever picked for England before him. He didn't fare too well in Pakistan in 1969 and I told him it was because his stance was getting lower and lower, so that he was looking *down* when the bowler delivered it. He was trying to *stop* the ball, rather than *play* it. I remember a very shrewd remark once from Roger at Wellingborough; I'd scraped a fifty against some high-class leg-spin by Mushtaq. I was feeling pretty pleased with myself at lunch-time when Roger came up to me and said, 'I won't say well played, Bas – but well *done*.' He only played three times for England and I managed that 44 times. I still can't work that out.

Tony Brown: He won games on his own for Gloucestershire for many seasons. He would soldier on all day, bowl his heart out and field magnificently. A clean striker of the ball, he often looked a very good batsman. A fit man and unlucky not to have played at least once for England; if he'd got in, his all-round qualities might have kept him in for years.

Mike Taylor: A thinking cricketer who's worked very hard for Hampshire. One of the quiet men of the game, he worked out his limitations a long time ago. He can bat attractively and keep an end up if necessary. A reliable medium-paced bowler. Worse cricketers have played for England in my time.

Of course, the crucial thing to assess when you're talking about England potential is character. You assume that these are all good players, that they have the abilities to do well in representative cricket. But could they cope with Test Match pressures? Have they got that indefinable Test Match temperament? I've seen many fine players simply freeze when they turn out for England, while on the other hand men like John Snow and Tony Greig could look mediocre at county level and thrive in the big Test Match atmosphere. It's always a fascinating exercise picking the 'nearly men' – and believe me, county cricketers all do it – but you never know how these blokes will perform for their country until the chips are down, the crowd are baying for blood and there's a big, hulking brute of a fast bowler waiting at the far end.

13 Looking Back

Since I retired many friends and cricket lovers have said to me, 'It was a good time to go, Bas. The game's not as enjoyable as it was.' Well, I don't agree. The game is certainly more tense now and the increased money to be made tends to concentrate some players' minds a little more – but I find there's still the same good fellowship and humour in English cricket. Much of this is to do with the high quality of umpiring, and the hard school that the players come through. Most county cricketers are taken under the wing of a few senior players when they first come into the side; they're told what to do, and more importantly, what *not* to do. In county cricket there's still a code of conduct that is usually observed – the number of competitions means that teams can often play each other four times a season and nobody wants grudges to be carried over a period of weeks. The fact that many county cricketers have played against each other for years helps smooth out most tensions – and there's always the bar afterwards.

It *is* true, though, that cricket is taking more out of the players than it used to. The extra money leads to a more competitive instinct and that means the fitness demands are greater. In my last few years in the game, I noticed a few things that bothered me on the field, even though they were very much in the minority. We played a Benson and Hedges match against Somerset which was a very close contest and passions got a little high. With about five overs to go, they needed twenty to win with just two wickets left; young Greg Watson bowled to Graham Burgess who slashed it just behind point where Norman Gifford caught it. Graham turned to go but then moved back again, so Norman said, 'I've caught it, Graham.' Graham stood his ground, Norman confirmed to the umpire Alan Whitehead that he'd caught the ball but he was given not out. Greg Watson said to Burgess, 'You've played against this guy for long enough now – surely if he said it was out, it's out.' I thought that was a very significant remark from a young Australian in his first season in county cricket;

he'd heard about the camaraderie of English cricket, yet it was almost like being back in Australia, where nobody walks.

Then there was the time when we were playing Kent at home. The wicket at Worcester was turning and Derek Underwood bowled to me; it bounced, hit me on the thigh and went through to Alan Knott. The close fielders all went up in a loud appeal just as I was turning to say, 'Come off it' – I was sure they'd seen it hit my thigh. I looked down the wicket and I was given out. I was livid, and at the end of the day I was sitting in my usual seat on the balcony when my old mate Knotty came out. 'Cheerio, Giffie,' he said to Norman, 'I'm sorry about Bas.' Norman was equally annoyed and he said, 'It's no good saying sorry to me, talk to Bas.' And I blurted out, 'I don't want to know, Knotty – as a matter of fact, I'm watching King Kong on the box tonight and I'm sure *that'll* be more fun.' It sounds irrational and irrelevant in cold print, I agree, but I was angry at being dismissed in such a way. I could not believe that there could be any mistake.

Incidents like those two are rare, I assure you – but there is a barely discernible trend which I'm sure the umpires will start cracking down on very soon. But when someone's dubious action comes within the framework of the rules, that's the time to worry. That's what happened in that amazing Benson and Hedges match with Somerset when their skipper Brian Rose caused such a fuss when he declared after just one over to qualify for the quarter finals. How could a captain think of doing something like that? I felt so sorry for all those people who'd paid good money to witness a farce, those schoolchildren who'd come to see class players. When I heard the rumour in the morning, I said, 'They couldn't possibly do that.' I knew they were on the phone to Lord's seeking a ruling but I thought the spirit of the game, rather than the letter of the law, would prevail. I wonder if they would have done the same thing when the TV cameras were present the day before ? It was right to expel Somerset from the Benson and Hedges Cup that season and if they felt like martyrs, they should think about the customers who pay their wages. Luckily the storm of protest was so great that I believe any other team tempted to sharp practice – even though it's within the letter of the law – has been warned off.

One of the reasons why I'm optimistic that the game will continue to be played properly in England is the continuing high standard of umpiring. When I started, men like Sid Butler, Charlie Elliott, Arthur Fagg and John Langridge didn't stand much nonsense and today umpires of the calibre of 'Dickie' Bird, Ken Palmer and David Constant are just as fair-minded and strict when necessary. It's a hard life for them and we sometimes forget when a decision goes against us that they have to be concentrating all day, even though none of them are youngsters. Now that the money is getting better for first-class umpires, more ex-players are coming on to the list and that must be good for the game. A former player knows the tricks of the trade, who to watch out for and who to trust – and the players respond to that. It's not so good abroad, I'm afraid. Overseas umpires are only amateurs; there isn't enough first-class cricket around to improve their judgement. I know they stand in a lot of high-class club cricket but there's no substitute for hard, concentrated work at any job and these chaps often have their own jobs to go to during the week. On the last England tour to Australia, one of the umpires was standing in his first Test after umpiring in just three first-class matches. With all due respect to that umpire, that's hardly the ideal preparation for a Test. Of course, that doesn't justify the kind of nonsense some of the West Indians and Australians have been getting up to in recent Tests; any player who runs into an umpire or kicks the stumps over should not only be suspended, he should be hit where it hurts most – in the pocket. The overseas players *never* try that on in England, because they know they just can't get away with it.

This may sound strange coming from an overseas player, but I think there are too many of them in English cricket and the authorities are right to start limiting their numbers. Originally the idea of signing a star overseas player to boost the county game was a good one but it went haywire when too many mediocre ones were signed up and the young English cricketers suffered. Not enough counties were making determined efforts to look for young talent on their own doorstep, it was too easy just to whip out the cheque book. The English batsmen weren't getting many chances to build an innings because many of the top four places in the batting order were taken up by overseas players. That's why we're now going through a phase where there are few English batsmen geared to Test cricket; it's not necessarily the fault of one-day cricket, it's more to do with lack of opportunity at the start of an innings.

I've always been against giving an overseas player a benefit after his ten years with a county. I think it's right that he should be paid well, that he should have all the extra perks like free air travel for himself and his wife and free accommodation – but he'll be making money all the year round simply because he's a cricket mercenary, while the England player who carries on quietly with the job and does just as much for his county over a decade earns nowhere near as much money. It's that kind of player – an Alan Ormrod, a David Shepherd, a Mike Harris – who deserves a bumper benefit at the end of his loyal service rather than the overseas player who'll never go short.

I also believe it's wrong for an overseas player to captain a county. I know men like Procter and Barlow have worked wonders for the counties they played for but I don't believe someone from Adelaide, Natal or Christchurch has the same gut feeling for his adopted county as a local lad. A county captain should carry the flag throughout the winter as well. He should go round the circuit of club cricket dinners and badger the players to come to see the county. He should encourage a feeling of local pride. An overseas player can't do that because he's busy earning his corn a few thousand miles away. And an English county captain is important for the development of England's Test team. The selectors should have as many candidates as possible to pick from when they're looking for the next England skipper. Look at the field now – it's not exactly brimful of alternatives, is it?

I suppose the biggest revolution in my time was caused by Kerry Packer. I don't think Packer did as much for the English county cricketer as many of his supporters claim. Our own Players Association has done more than anybody for the players in England; the blokes who run that are all reasonable people who know just how much cash the counties can afford. They were directly involved in the negotiations for a minimum wage for county cricketers and any influence exerted by the coffers of Kerry Packer was purely circumstantial. The hard work needed to get a county cricketer an acceptable wage was done by the Players Association, not by an organisation based in Sydney.

To be honest I probably would have signed for Packer if such a thing had been around in my day and I was good enough to be selected. But I wouldn't have wanted my cake both ways, like many of the World Series Cricket stars. My attitude is, 'If you sign for Packer, that's fine and good luck but don't expect to play again for your country.' It was Test cricket that made these players into big stars and marketable commodities and once they'd turned their back on it, they shouldn't have been brought back to play again in Tests. Test cricket is important – a third of a county player's salary is paid for by Test Match receipts, so it's vital to keep Tests strong and healthy. If you lose the appeal of Test cricket by creaming off all the star players, then you also weaken the county game, cause the counties to draw in their financial horns and think about sacking a few players to make ends meet. So Packer's brand of cricket could never be said to be good for the English game.

I hear a lot of players say that they play too much cricket. I disagree; a county plays on average 23 first-class games a season and plenty of other limited over matches as well, but I don't think that's excessive. Ask any of the moaners what they wanted to be when kids and they'll reply, 'a professional cricketer.' They're getting paid to play the game they love and I only wish I'd come into it a lot earlier. Professional county cricketers who complain high-handedly that they're bored with the game are better out of it, in my opinion, irrespective of their talent.

I also disagree that the hundred-over limit on first innings of a county match is killing the game. I think it means a worthwhile game for players and spectators because after a good day's batting, you'll see their opening bowlers really slip themselves in the final hour, which is always a good sight. And if the captains are good enough, there's plenty of time to make a game out of it over three days. I don't think the overs limit has stunted the development of England batsmen, that's been caused by having too many overseas batsmen in county

cricket. Patience is needed by those who bemoan the lack of
class English batsmen. These things come in cycles – look at
England in 1969 after we'd lost so many great batsmen within
a couple of years. There'll be another May, another Dexter or
Cowdrey – it's just a matter of waiting.

When I look back on my time in the game, I wish I could
have played till I was 90. I loved the leg-pulling, the life of
travel, the fun of meeting people and old friends, the pleasure
of going into a pub anywhere in England and somebody saying to me, 'Aren't you Basil D'Oliveira? Come and have a
drink.' I've loved the English people, their decency, their
respect for privacy. I admire the traditions of England, the
continuity of a way of life that has so much to offer. A lot of
the tradition stems from the Royal Family and when I was
awarded the O.B.E. in 1969, I felt humble and overwhelmed
with gratitude and respect.

All the way down to Buckingham Palace, I kept thinking – what have I done to deserve this? There are far more
worthwhile people in life than a simple cricketer! My family
and I had a marvellous day at the Palace and I still smile at
Damian's reaction to the guards standing stock still outside the
Palace – 'they can't be alive, Dad, their eyes aren't moving!' I
was amazed at the precision of the operation – we started at
10.15 and finished bang on 12.15, as we'd been assured. The
Queen gave me my award, asked me about playing cricket all
the year round, wondered if I missed the sunshine, etc. I felt
unbelievable; I was the only coloured guy there as far as I
could see, standing beside a lot of terrific people who were
getting awards for bravery, and scientific achievements, and
I'm getting one for playing cricket! To end a proud day,
Naomi and I went to the West End to see a show. We were
sitting in a pub in Drury Lane just before the start and a man
came up to me and asked if I was really Basil D'Oliveira.
When I said yes, he congratulated me on my award and said, 'I
was right behind you this morning getting mine as well.' He
was from Philadelphia and he'd won it the previous year for
some scientific work but he had insisted on saving up and
coming over to receive it at Buckingham Palace! He just
wanted to tell his grandchildren that he'd met the Queen and
been inside the Palace: it was strange that, in all the pubs of

London, he and I should end up in the same one that night.

Another time when my cricketing name got me into high-powered company was at a cocktail party at 10 Downing Street. By this time, I thought, 'God, this is getting ridiculous', but I went along; George Best was there and Frankie Howerd, Robin Day and Kenny Lynch. Harold Wilson's press agent told me that the Prime Minister very much wanted to meet me, so I told him it would be a pleasure. The P.M. and I started chatting, I refused his offer of champagne, and he asked, 'What would you really like to drink, Basil?' I said 'a pint of beer', and he replied, 'Do you know, so would I'. A few minutes later, I was standing drinking a pint of beer with the Prime Minister of Britain, pinching myself, wondering when I'd wake up.

Perhaps the most memorable non-cricket day was my appearance on 'This Is Your Life' in 1971. Now I always watch that programme whenever possible because I think it's a moving, sentimental occasion and I'm a little bit like that anyway. But I used to say to Naomi, 'I'll never go on that if anyone ever asks you – I'd make a fool of myself.' Anyway, just before I flew out to Australia with the 1970/71 England side, my business adviser and friend, Reg Hayter, told me, 'Play well, Bas, there might be a nice surprise for you when you come back.' I hadn't a clue what he meant, so I thought no more of it. Well when we returned in triumph, Reg met me at the airport and said, 'Well done, I want you to come down to London on Monday to talk business.' This was on Thursday and I told Reg he must be joking. I was going to stay in Worcester with my family for a month. Reg told me that Naomi had approved the trip and I got mad then, because I thought my own family didn't want to see me! Naomi was also at the airport that Thursday and she told me she was quite happy for me to go down again to London so soon after arriving back. I couldn't make out what the hell was going on, I thought there was something very odd happening – especially as Naomi was ill all that weekend with stomach pains (she later told me it was the worry of keeping something from me for the first time in our lives).

Anyway, Reg Hayter pulled a master stroke because he told me he'd got tickets for the Henry Cooper/Joe Bugner

boxing match on the Tuesday; Reg knew I liked boxing and
that I would be tempted to change my mind about going
down to London. Unknown to me, Reg and the researcher for
'This is Your Life' had been at my home while I was playing
in Worcester; Naomi was helping them sort out the biographi-
cal stuff. All weekend, I was in a state of uncertainty about
going to London; it just didn't *feel* right. Anyway, to Naomi's
great relief, I left on the Monday afternoon – that meant she
could be picked up by brother, Ivan, who lived at Leicester,
then taken down to London to stay in a hotel with all my
family and friends who'd been flown over from South Africa.
But Naomi took the precaution of getting our home telephone
disconnected, in case anybody answered my call and blurted
out that she had gone to London. So I was phoning all Monday night, all next day and even from the press box at the big
fight on Tuesday night – but there was no reply from home,
in fact the phone had gone dead. I was out of my mind with
worry yet Reg kept saying, 'Don't worry, keep calm.' I was
getting madder and madder.

On the Wednesday Reg told me I had to be at Lord's at
six o'clock for an MCC dinner. I said, 'What for? I've done
my job in Australia, why bother me now?' Reg gave me some
flannel about it being a special dinner laid on to wish me well,
etc, etc. I was always susceptible to flattery! By this time I was
frantic with worry about Naomi and the kids and Reg also had
a problem – how to keep me sober. He and I always have a
few drinks when we meet up and as far as I was concerned,
this time was no different, provided I could find out what was
wrong at home. Reg said to me at lunchtime, 'I think we'll
have a Turkish bath, Basil.' That was the daftest idea I'd ever
heard from him, especially as El Vino's was open in Fleet
Street, where we often used to meet. He had a terrible time
persuading me to go to the RAC Club but finally I started
taking pity on him, I thought he was going round the twist. I
humoured him and Reg said we could stay in the bath till five
o'clock when my old mate, Peter Smith (now cricket writer
for the *Daily Mail*) would pick us up and drive us to Lord's. I
seriously started to doubt Reg's sanity when he told me he
was going to buy me a new shirt for the meeting at Lord's! I
kept telling him there was nothing wrong with my red shirt,

yet Reg swore blind that a nice, new white one would be better. Unknown to me, the TV boys had told Naomi to get me in a white shirt because red wouldn't look good on the screen – that's one little ploy of theirs that failed.

So we got to the RAC Club and had a sauna and Reg took an eternity getting dressed. 'Reg, come on', I said, 'you're like a bloody old woman, what's up with you?' By this time, it was only 4.30 and he could see I was getting distinctly fed up, and that I was also distinctly sober. Yet, just to waste a little more time, the following conversation ensued:

'Basil, tell me about your father'
'What the hell for? Are you feeling all right?'
'Just talk a little about your father'
'But Reg, we never talk about my father, we always talk sport'

I was beginning to think he was certifiable but what he was trying to do was to jog my memory for the programme that night – and also waste some precious minutes. By this time, it was five o'clock and Peter Smith turned up to take us to Lord's for the appointed hour of six. By 5.20, we were very near the Clarendon Court Hotel at Edgware Road, where all the county cricketers stay and I wanted to pop in to see some of our friends behind the bar and in the restaurant. Peter stopped for petrol. I noticed that his tank was half-full, but he said he needed to fill up for a long journey. He stood chatting for five more minutes with the forecourt attendant and I was getting very restless. Peter and Reg were still trying to kill time – and to keep me away from the Clarendon Court Hotel, because all the England tour party would probably be there having a drink before going to the TV studios for the programme.

I was dying for a drink now and they agreed to stop. They took me to the dingiest pub I've ever seen, where we sat drinking gins and tonics. I was convinced I was the only sane man round the table by that time – a conviction that strengthened when we got to Lord's and they both dashed out of the car before I could catch my breath. So I sat back and thought, 'That's a fine couple of friends I've got here – I'm stuck in the dark and don't know what the hell's going on.' They'd gone ahead to warn Eamonn Andrews and the rest that we'd arrived. We walked in, I said hello to a few MCC officials and then Eamonn Andrews turned around and said, 'This is Your Life'. Well, I could have died; in that old cliché, you could have knocked me down with a feather. After I'd recovered from the shock and brandished a friendly fist at Reg and Peter, I had to break the news to Eamonn; I wasn't going on the show. Eamonn said would I please come in the car with him to the studios and that if I was still adamant, he wouldn't press me. There was just an hour to go and poor old Eamonn was obviously sweating inside. We got to the studio at 6.40 and Eamonn got out of the car with these words, 'Basil, I respect your wishes – but once you find out who's inside that studio, you'll be an awfully disappointed man if you turn me down.' A shrewd move, that. I pondered my fate for five minutes, then a girl researcher came out and said, 'Are you coming in, Mr D'Oliveira?' I agreed and it felt worse than walking out to face the Aussies at Melbourne. After a large, stiff drink, the show was under way and I loved it, even though I was sure I'd break down and cry. John Arlott was there and from South Africa there was Benny Bansda, my sister, my parents and other friends. John Kay walked in, and Mr and Mrs Lord, my friends from Middleton – it was a very warm, sentimental occasion. And it was topped off by one little piece of film.

When they researched the programme they asked Naomi if I'd like to see one particular thing that I've always missed. Well, she and my sons still went to church, even though I'd lapsed by that time. I was nevertheless very proud that Damian and Shaun sang in the church choir, even though I'd never seen that. Naomi told the researcher that it would be lovely to see my two boys in their cassocks singing in the church choir. They went down to their school, told the headmistress they were filming a documentary on school choirs and got permission to film in the church. But Damian and Shaun weren't told the real reason for the film, because they would probably have let the cat out of the bag. So the film director had to make sure that my two sons led the choir out when it was time to shoot the film! I was knocked out when I saw that piece of film, I was so proud. A good job the programme was nearly at an end because I was ready to fold up.

Incidentally, the boys didn't know I was on the TV until Barbara, our next-door neighbour, called them into her house at 7 o'clock to watch the show.

I couldn't get over the secrecy involved, the amount of planning. All my family in South Africa had to get permission to have some time off work but they couldn't give the real reason, in case it was leaked to the South African press and then it would get out over here. My family weren't even allowed out of their hotel in London, because of the rare chance that they might bump into me in the street! So if anyone ever tells you that 'This is Your Life' is a bit of a hoax, don't you believe it.

There are so many memories . . . There was the time Roy Booth and I had a few drinks in a club at Yeovil when we were playing Somerset. That night, Worcestershire were well and truly in the cart and we had no chance of hanging on, with the ball turning all over the place. So Roy and I tried to drown our sorrows and somebody started chirping up in the bar, telling us that Somerset were a great side. Just for a laugh I said, 'We won't lose this game tomorrow.' It was daft considering we only had four wickets left and we were thousands of runs behind. Bravado took over yet again and I found myself betting him a fiver that we'd draw the game – and a fiver was a lot in 1967. By the time we left the club, Roy and I were pretty happy, and we lost our way getting back to the hotel. Then we found we were locked out. It was four o'clock in the morning and Roy said, 'I'm senior pro, so you'll have to go up the drainpipe and let me in.' Up I went and we finally got to bed. I was rooming with him and a few hours later, we were lying in bed feeling our sore heads and reality was slowly dawning about the job in hand on the cricket pitch. That's when Roy reminded me that I bet a bloke a fiver we'd save the match. Not only that – I'd bet him I'd score a hundred! I nearly fell out of bed and told him I didn't remember a thing about that, which was true. Out we went and as luck would have it, we were the not-out batsmen. I couldn't escape from Roy's clutches all that day! We'd meet in mid-wicket after Brian Langford's off-breaks had bamboozled us in the previous over and say things like – 'How are you?' 'Bloody awful. What about you?' 'Worse than that. I think I'm going to die.'

All stirring stuff – but I got my hundred, 147 not out to be precise. A hell of a long day's cricket it was, and I don't know how I got through it. We drew the match and a fortnight later, I got a note from the mysterious punter from the club bar, saying 'Well done, here's your £5. I think we could make a habit of this.' Not on your life. I aged two years when Boothie broke the news to me that morning.

I'll miss the by-play in the middle, particularly Jimmy Cumbes' leg-pulling and Norman Gifford's deadpan wit. When I think of Giffie, I'll think of the time he set up Fred Titmus at Lord's. Giffie ran in twice to bowl at him and on each occasion, just as he was about to deliver, Fred backed away, saying he wasn't quite ready. Now Giffie has a low boiling point on occasions and he was getting narked. At the third time of asking, he spotted a plane going overhead, paused in his run-up and shouted, 'Incidentally, Fred – is that plane bothering you?' That brought the house down.

All my life I've been guided by some strange hand of fate. I'm not a religious man, but I believe in God and I'm sure that something or somebody has guided me through life and taken me in certain directions at crucial moments. I always thought of myself as a cricketer who got away with murder; why should I get wickets with my bowling? How could I hold down a place in the England team with men like Roger Prideaux on the sidelines? It's unreal, there's no logic in it. Just think of the luck that I've had – Wes Hall making himself unavailable for Middleton at the last minute, John Arlott taking up my case, the article in *World Sports* that appeared at just the right time, the advice from Eric Price when I wanted to go home in 1960, the kick up the backside from Charlie Hallows when I was struggling at Worcester in 1964. What about that nick to the West Indian keeper second ball in my Test debut? The fact that I missed out on the Old Trafford debacle in 1966, the bowling of Alan Dixon that persuaded Colin Cowdrey to keep me in mind for the Oval Test of 1968, the illness of Roger Prideaux and the injuries of Barry Knight and Tom Cartwright that led to the tour being called off in September 1968. The chain of circumstances is so long and tortuous that it can't just be circumstantial.

Now the wheel has come full circle and I'm no longer a

player. It seems unthinkable yet I recall the words of Colin Cowdrey to me during the dark days of September 1968. 'Cricket is only a stepping stone in your life. You'll go on to other things eventually.' Perhaps he's right. Perhaps it's time I devoted my attentions to South Africa.

14 The South African Question

In the autumn of 1961, I was going back to Cape Town by boat with my wife and young son after another season with Middleton. We'd been at sea for about four days when I decided to take a stroll on deck before dinner. A Rhodesian couple came up to me and congratulated me on my behaviour and that of my wife and year-old son. They said that after many years acceptance of apartheid, they now realized it was wrong and that there was no real difference between them and us.

Then in 1976 I found myself in Israel, playing and coaching with a club side from Harrow. I was sitting one night in the bar with my team-mates when a South African asked us if we were all English – 'because,' he said while pointing at me, 'I know he's not English because he's the one who stopped us playing Test cricket.' With that, he swallowed his drink and stormed out.

I mention these two incidents to show how my attitude has changed towards race relations. In 1961, I was grateful for praise from any white person and I was subservient to that Rhodesian couple who were surprised that Damian was well-behaved and that Naomi was tidily dressed and decent. Today, if that happened, I'd be angry; I'd feel insulted that any remarks were needed just because my family behaved like any civilized family, irrespective of colour. I would feel patronized. But in 1976, I just laughed at the misguided South African in that Israeli bar; I could see he had so much hate in his soul that nothing I said would make him change his mind. A few years earlier, I would have been deeply hurt and shocked; but my confidence and self-respect had grown over the years and I knew in my heart that I had always done my best to foster good race relations.

Those two incidents were on my mind when I accepted an invitation to join a Sports Council delegation to South Africa in January 1980. The four-man delegation headed by the former England rugby international Dickie Jeeps, was going out there to assess the progress of multi-racial sport in the Republic. We were told we weren't out there to make recommendations, simply to gather as many facts as possible and then report back to the Sports Council in Britain. I felt a duty to accept the invitation, not simply out of personal interest and the desire to be better-informed but because sport had done so much for me that it was only right that I should try to do something for sport and sportsmen of all colours and beliefs.

I was determined to approach the task with an open mind. I don't suppose many would blame me for having a hatred of Mr Vorster and the Nationalist Government for the events of 1968 but I have never felt that way; the thing was much bigger than me and once I knew I couldn't control the situation, I felt simply sadness, never hatred. I knew from my visits to South Africa over the years that things were improving, that more and more non-white sportsmen were being integrated with whites, and I was looking forward to getting nearer the truth than ever before. After all, we were due to meet Cabinet Ministers, many sports organizations and interested persons. Surely I would be able to see things in a clearer perspective after this trip?

I saw much that was extremely encouraging and I have to admit the changes that had taken place were so great that I wouldn't have believed them possible in my time. Ten years ago, I would have said that the Nationalist Government was so entrenched in its attitude that any changes would be extremely minor and very gradual. I'm delighted to admit that forecast would have been over-pessimistic. But my own personal view about isolating South Africa from international sport has not changed. I still feel isolation should continue for just a few more years.

There is a chink in the armour of the Government's apartheid policies – and this has been caused by the isolation policy practised in other countries after the D'Oliveira Affair. There is an encouraging wind of change blowing through South Africa and I see nothing to stop that momentum, not even the opposition that Prime Minister Botha is now facing from right-wingers within his own Cabinet. But this thawing of attitude has been brought about by isolation, a fact confirmed privately to us by Cabinet Ministers and 'Mr Rugby' himself, Danie Craven. South Africa is a sport-mad country and they are so desperate to re-enter the world of international sport that another short period of isolation will, in my opinion, help the cause of non-racialism.

One of the fundamental things to emerge from our visit was that although multi-racial sport is advancing all the time, nevertheless apartheid still is practised off the sports field. The black cricketer may be able to compete on an equal level with whites on the cricket field but when the game's over, he reverts to being a black man when he travels home in a blacks-only train compartment. So a black man is equal for a few hours on a Saturday yet for the rest of the week, is unequal. Can this be right? That point was confirmed by Mr Dave Dalling, an Opposition MP in the South African Parliament, who told us, 'Sport is one of the few areas of South African life where there have been major changes.' I made a point of taking a walk round the cities on my own whenever possible on the Sports Council trip and I could still see the manifestations of apartheid; in Johannesburg, for instance, I saw again the segregated toilets and restaurants at both the airport and the train station. It all reminded me of the faces of my relatives whenever any of them come over to England to visit us. They all tend to look the same as I wait for them at London Airport. They've travelled in a non-segregated plane and when they arrive, they're worried and troubled by all the freedom that stares them in their faces. They take a long time to get used to the fact that English people won't hassle you because of your colour; they expect to be refused entry to various places. I felt the same way when I arrived in England twenty years ago – confused, hardly daring to believe certain basic freedoms are actually available. That haunted feeling is the product of apartheid. Can that system *really* be right?

The dilemma of the isolation policy is the obvious one –when to end it. If it was halted now, the Nationalist Government might think, 'Right, we've done enough, there's no need to carry out any other reforms. We're respectable again in the eyes of the world.' On the other hand, if it is continued, the influential South Africans might dig their heels in and refuse to move any further towards a non-racial society. This problem was recognized in a moving speech to the delegation by Mr R. W. J. Opperman, the President of the South African Olympic and National Games Association, in which he begged us to recommend easing the isolation policy and to work towards South Africa's re-entry to international sport. He said, 'I implore you: criticise us as much as you like but don't leave us with nothing to show as a result of your visit. Sport is the one medium that can bring the people of this land together on the basis of a broad South African patriotism. For the sake of sport – not for political or commercial reasons, show you are prepared to stand up and be counted.' He also told us that apartheid was being broken down at ten times the rate at which it was sometimes built up and that such progress was so far advanced that it could not be stopped.

Another man spelt out the dangers of the isolation policy to us – the Minister of Sport, Mr Punt Janson. He said that all nations have their pride and that if the outside world continued to ignore South Africa's progress towards multi-racial sport, then the South African reaction would be 'Go to hell'. He continued, 'A boycott is not likely to improve conditions, especially for the less privileged. To encourage enthusiasm in sport competitions among different peoples is essential. South Africans are a proud people and if boycotts continue, there could be a counter-productive reaction.' He pledged that South Africa would continue to provide the necessary amenities as fast as possible for as many as possible.

Such statements from the Minister of Sport about extra facilities for all colours are encouraging – but they still blur what is a vital issue. Sport and politics *do* mix, whether the politicians and sportsmen like it or not. As Bernard Atha, one of the delegation put it, 'Sport cannot be divorced from the environment in which it takes place.' My own experience in 1968 proved that. It's because of political reasons that South Africa has been isolated in the sporting world.

It's because of politics that I can't dance with Eddie Barlow's wife after a cricket match unless the authority staging the match has a special permit. It's because of politics that Omar Henry, a Muslem, was barred from a restaurant in Cape Town on New Year's Eve, even though he was going inside to have a meal with his white colleagues from the Western

Province side he'd played for that day. It's because of politics that black children are sadly lacking in educational and sporting opportunities. And to those South Africans who deplore the fusion of sport and politics, I say this – remember the 1977 rugby tour of your country by a World side. Your Government was so delighted that so many great rugby players had made the trip that your Sports Minister remarked that the tour proved that South Africa didn't stand alone, that it still had friends. Surely that's a classic case of mixing politics with sport? And what about Mrs Thatcher's disapproval of a British Olympic team attending the Moscow Games because of Russia's invasion of Afghanistan?

It's true that the various laws which prevent people of different colours from mixing before and after a sports event are gradually being ignored. Usually an application for a permit is enough to decree things that the British would take for granted – for example, a black man having a drink with his white colleague after their team has just won a match, or non-whites allowed to come into a dance, or even dance with whites. Legislation like the Liquor Act, and the Group Areas Act (designed to prevent non-racial socializing) still exist, but many clubs and ground authorities turn a blind eye. But the mere fact that a permit has to be applied for still rankles with non-whites. On our Sports Council trip, everyone wanted to talk about the recent Omar Henry incident; the pro-Government people we met pointed out that any embarrassment to Henry would have been avoided if he'd rung the appropriate department in Pretoria, which is manned 24 hours a day to deal with permits. But the mere fact that Henry would have to ask *permission* to join his team-mates at a meal is appalling. And would that department in Pretoria be open on New Year's Eve? The incident so angered Henry's captain, Eddie Barlow, that he boycotted Cape Town restaurants for the rest of the season and refused to see our delegation, pointing out that nothing had changed for the better in recent years. I could understand the anger of Eddie Barlow – a man who has consistently and genuinely worked for multi-racial sport over the years – but there's no doubt that a hell of a lot *has* been done, far more than I realized. But the crunch is coming. The Prime Minister, Mr Pieter Botha, has said that it's high time non-whites weren't treated like lepers, and I believe he is a reformist. In 1979, he pledged a relaxation in the Immorality Act and the Mixed Marriages Act, the laws which forbid inter-racial sex, and if he can get those altered, the climate will be altered beneficially. He has problems within his own Cabinet but I was encouraged after our meeting with Dr Koornhof, the Minister of Co-operation and Development. He told us that South Africa was committed to doing away with hurtful racial discrimination and that he had appointed an officer to scan all the laws so that various statutes could be removed. He conceded that the Government had to move away from the image of being 'pig-headed, hard-hearted and unemotional'.

But the feeling persists that the Government is relaxing the legislation simply *as it applies to sport,* not to the rest of society. And the fact remains that an unco-operative local authority or policeman can still insist on the strict letter of the law being observed. This is why the South African Council of Sport refuse to co-operate with the Government until the laws of the land are changed. The President of SACOS, Mr Hassan Howa, is a man I admire; I don't think he has all that high an opinion of me, though. He sees me as a bit of an 'Uncle Tom' because I won't join him in an all-out policy of non co-operation. I respect him, because he has been consistent throughout in his views on non-racialism in sport as well as society in general. But Mr Howa wasn't particularly warm in his support of the Sports Council's visit; the slogan of SACOS is 'No normal sport in an abnormal society' and Mr Howa was at great pains to impress this point on the delegation. He felt Dickie Jeeps was a little too pro-Government, a view which I reject, and he told us that the present policy towards sport was little more than a cosmetic exercise. He told us, 'How can blacks compete on equal terms and then be humiliated by the apartheid laws off the field?' and that until more money was poured into non-white education, there would always be a system of apartheid. 'In a white school, every child must play sport; whereas the black child probably has no shoes to wear to school.' Much of what Mr Howa says is undeniably true; my argument is that he goes too far along the road of rigidity. SACOS is an important body, it's the non-racial organization dealing with 17 national sports bodies – but its attitude towards participation with whites is as dogmatic as any Afrikaaner from the Orange Free State. Mr Howa maintains that any non-white sportsman affiliated to bodies other than SACOS is either a stooge of the white Establishment, somebody whose livelihood depends on co-operation with the whites, or simply a well-intentioned but deluded person. Now I disagree with that, although I also disagree with the view expressed to us by Dr Koornhof that SACOS simply uses sport for political ends. I've had my ups and downs with Mr Howa in the past – beginning in 1958 when he was manager of a Coloureds side I skippered in an inter-racial tournament in Cape Town and I had to tell him to stop interfering in the running of the team. But I've always respected his views; I accepted his advice in 1972 and 1977 when I'd been invited to play in matches that I thought would help non-racial sport. In 1972 I was due to partner Tony Greig in a double wicket competition in South Africa. I thought it would help topple a few more barriers if I was seen partnering a white South African but Mr Howa thought that would be provocative to the non-whites, that it might have looked that I'd 'sold out' to the white man. Of course, I disagreed but I accepted his advice because after all, he was closer to the opinions of more non-whites than I was. Then in 1977, Eddie Barlow wanted me to play for Western Province against Transvaal at Newlands. I dearly wanted to play at Newlands but Hassan Howa again thought the time wasn't right.

I suppose Mr Howa and I will always pursue the same goal from different angles but I do feel he is inconsistent in one respect. In 1977 he wrote a very revealing couple of sentences in a splendid book called *Cricket in Isolation* by Andre Odendaal which dealt with the inter-relation between sport and politics in South Africa. In his own chapter, Hassan Howa wrote that 'One man vote is wrong for South Africa. With approximately 20 million Africans and 4 million other people, it cannot work, it cannot be a viable proposition'. How can he be serious? How can you say that 'one man, one vote' is wrong to the Africans who live in Soweto or New Brighton in Port Elizabeth or Langa in Cape Town? Will there be a special vote for the Coloureds, a special one for the whites –

and nothing for the blacks? Is Mr Howa saying that the blacks are too unintelligent to appreciate having the right to vote? Surely Mr Howa – a man of mixed blood himself – is advocating apartheid in reverse here?

The attitude of the Sports Council delegation from black militants was basically: 'You say you're not going to make recommendations, so why bother coming out here in the first place?' Well, we weren't empowered to make recommendations to anybody, we simply wanted to get at the facts and then present them to the Sports Council for their consumption. And the most revealing set of statistics I came across concerned education. It was quite clear that non-white children were still lagging behind when it came to Government spending. These are the latest figures available. They cover the 1976/77 financial year.

	Expenditure per head	Teacher/pupil ratio	Total enrolment
White	R 644	1/20	942,000
Coloured	R 140	1/30	688,000
Indian	R 190	1/27	195,000
African	R 42	1/52	3,898,000

So it's clear that not enough is being done for schoolchildren of all races – and this, I believe, is the area that should be tackled as a priority. Equality of opportunity is the aim and if the schools are properly integrated, there will be peace in South Africa. I know it will take a long time and that many white parents will be reluctant to co-operate – but if only the kids can grow up in the right frame of mind there can be a well-ordered, non-racial society. Kids don't care about colour bars; watch them at a party, all they're interested is in cream cakes and balloons. They're not dogged by the hang-ups of their elders. As they get older, they can integrate in the same sports team, share each other's successes and failures and gradually beat down the barriers of bias.

It's because of this lack of equal opportunity that I don't feel all that sorry for the great South African cricketers who've missed out on Test careers. I never had a Test career with my own country, either – I had to come halfway round the world to get one. I missed out because there were no real opportunities for people with my colour of skin. It annoys me when I read about what a great side the Springboks of the 'seventies would have been; it would have been an even *greater* side if it had been the product of a society where everyone had the same chance to stake his claim for a place. I wonder how many Procters, Richards and Pollocks are to be found in the black townships? I won't have anybody questioning the integrity of the white South African cricketers who've made many courageous gestures towards non-racial sport, but I don't see why I should feel sorry that they've missed out on displaying their talents to a wider audience. That fate has been experienced by non-whites for centuries in South Africa.

I don't believe there is one white sportsman who won't now admit that South Africa's expulsion from Test cricket was deserved at the time. I know many were absolutely sickened by the events of 1968, and by other incidents as well. Time after time on my Sports Council trip, people came up to me and apologized for the past. Cabinet Ministers told us, 'We don't want to make the same mistake again,' and even though they didn't spell it out, I knew they were referring to the D'Oliveira Affair. I didn't meet one white person who was opposed to change – and that included three Cabinet Ministers. I'm convinced that if my case arose today, South Africa would not take the kind of steps that led to its expulsion from Test cricket in 1970. The recurring words I heard in January 1980 was 'gradual'; everybody accepts that change is coming to South Africa and the only doubt is the speed at which it is achieved. I believe that in about ten years' time, there will be several black players good enough to play for South Africa. At the moment, Omar Henry – a fine, accurate left-arm spinner – is the only one who could challenge for a place in the national side on merit because the facilities for non-white sportsmen have not been good enough in the past. But they are getting better and soon the improved coaching and sterner competition will throw up excellent black cricketers in the same way that it's happened to black footballers in Britain.

It remains to be seen whether South Africa will be playing Test cricket within the next decade. My own view is that there's a lot of talking still to be done before the hostile members of the International Cricket Conference agree to bury the hatchet. When South Africa was thrown out of Test cricket in 1970, the Cricket Council ruled that re-entry was conditional on teams being chosen on a multi-racial basis in South Africa. That condition has been solidly met with the formation of the South African Cricket Union in 1977 – it meant that at last just one official national body was in control of South African cricket, organized outside the apartheid framework and framed with non-racial principles. All discrimination on race, creed or colour for cricketing purposes was outlawed by SACU, so for the first time, cricketers of all races could play the game together.

But that is not enough for India, the West Indies and Pakistan; these member countries of the International Cricket Conference refuse to consider resumption of Test cricket with South Africa until apartheid is removed from all walks of South African life. The views of these three countries are decisive; there is now a delicate balance between the pro and anti-South Africa factions within the ICC so the matter is left permanently in limbo. All I can say to the 'anti' faction is that they should take a look at the progress made in South Africa at first hand; they will be amazed. I do not disagree with any continuance of the policy of isolation but I do feel that the critics of South Africa should come and see things in the flesh, rather than just rely on second-hand opinions and distorted press coverage.

Sport remains the *only* hope of bringing the people of South Africa together – but what is the South African Government's official policy towards sport? That's something our delegation could not ascertain, despite repeated requests to the Government for a clarification. In 1976, the then Sports Minister, Dr Koornhof, said the official policy was that all the ethnic groups must play under their own separate jurisdictions, in other words, non-racial sport was still out. But since then, although massive changes have taken place in sport, the Nationalist Government won't update their policy. It's clear that the reformists in the Cabinet fear a backlash from the reactionaries if the issue is clarified, so the policy of 'nudge, nudge, wink, wink' continues.

I don't believe that complete change will come until the game of rugby puts its house in order in South Africa. Rugby is the sporting god over there; cricket is simply an Englishman's game in comparison. Attitudes in rugby circles are entrenched towards non-racialism, as in states like the Orange Free State or Northern Transvaal, and it was clear from our investigations that sports like cricket, athletics and boxing had done a lot more towards integration than rugby. The Opposition spokesman on sport, Mr Dave Dalling, told us that rugby had gone only about *a third* of the way down the road to being non-racial. Unlike cricket, there is not yet one controlling rugby body, there are three – for blacks, Coloureds and whites. We were told that one body was the next step.

Make no mistake about it – if the rugby citadel falls to the non-racial policy, that will be the beginning of the end for apartheid in South Africa. Rugby is the religion of many Afrikaaners, who are the bastions of the apartheid system. The area to concentrate on is in the Orange Free State and Northern Transvaal which is not only the heartland for apartheid but also for rugby. They don't even *think* about playing against non-whites there. Topple one entrenched belief and the other one will also fall, believe me.

I hope the British Lions rugby tour party didn't miss a trick to hammer home the gospel of non-racialism when they toured South Africa in the summer of 1980 because many Springbok rugby fanatics I talked to earlier in the year thought the tour signified acceptance of the apartheid system, that South Africa was being respectabilized by the resumption of tours. Things were at a fever pitch in the Republic when it was announced that the tour was going ahead and I hope the Lions players realized they were going on a political trip, not strictly a sporting trip. I sincerely trust the players and officials didn't miss a chance to ram some unpleasant facts down the throats of the diehards and the Government spokesmen. They should have said that apartheid is wrong, that it should be changed. Words like that from an international rugby player should make the traditionalists sit up and take notice. Many sportsmen are selfish and try to bury their heads in the sand; they take shelter behind the cliché, 'I'll play sport against anybody', but this recent Lions tour was different. I hope they were properly briefed by the Sports Council before they left for South Africa, because there could be no hope of them just settling down to talk rugby throughout the tour – and if they *did* pass up the opportunities to speak their minds, then they will have done non-racial sport a grave disservice.

Contrary to misinformed press reports at the time, I was against the Lions tour. I thought another spell of isolation was necessary, particularly for a sport which is so obsessional in South Africa. Unfortunately my feelings were misinterpreted by the chairman of the Sports Council at a press conference in London which I missed because my car broke down on the way from Worcester. It was stated that I was in favour of the Lions tour. This was not true; what I *would* have said was that the tour was a 'fait accompli' and so there was little point in opposing it. The British rugby authorities clearly weren't interested in our opinions as fact-finders because they confirmed that the tour would go ahead just a few days before our work started in January 1980. That was an incredible decision to me. Surely they could have waited until we'd returned after a fact-finding mission lasting just three weeks? I was in Cape Town when I heard the news and many blacks said to me, 'There's no point in your delegation coming over here, all your minds are made up in Britain without bothering to see things at first hand.'

This is not the time for closed minds on either side of the fence. The Nationalist Government must hammer out a sports policy that also gives an undertaking that non-racialism won't just apply to sport, Hassan Howa must try to dilute attitudes that are as rigid and unyielding as any rugby-loving Afrikaaner, the sportsmen must keep hammering at the Government's door to persuade them to open up their society. Those laws which degrade non-whites should be repealed and the farce of the permit system should be altered, thereby putting an official seal of approval on the policy of turning a blind eye. A black man can't be a white man during a day's sport and then revert to being a black man.

There is still a long way to go. Let no one doubt that it's taken isolation to get things moving towards a fairer society. The diehards mustn't now assume that enough has been done, yet they must also be encouraged. Perhaps in time I shall be back for good in my own country, trying in my own way to bring people of all colours closer together. If that happens, I shall always offer Britain as my model example of the kind of decent, multi-racial society any country should be proud to copy.

Statistical Survey

By Robert Brooke,
Association of Cricket Statisticians

1 Batting in First-class Cricket: Season by Season

Season	Where played	Mtchs	Inns	n.o.	Runs	h.s.	Av'ge	100s	50s	0s	ct
1962/62	Rhodesia	2	4	1	93	51	31.00	–	1	–	2
1962/63	Rhodesia	2	4	0	94	45	23.50	–	–	–	–
1963/64	Pakistan	5	7	2	261	115	52.20	1	1	1	2
1964	England	5	8	2	370	119	61.67	2	2	–	7
1964/65	Rhodesia	2	4	0	119	73	29.75	–	1	–	3
1965	England	31	45	6	1691	163	43.36	6	7	2	39
1965/66	Jamaica	1	2	0	110	101	55.00	1	–	–	–
1966	England	28	45	5	1536	126	38.40	2	11	2	23
1966/67	Barbados	1	2	0	21	16	10.50	–	–	–	–
1967	England	28	44	8	1618	174*	44.94	6	6	1	28
1967/68	West Indies	11	16	6	401	68*	40.10	–	3	2	5
1968	England	28	43	6	1223	158	33.05	2	7	4	23
1968/69	Ceylon & Pakistan	6	6	3	281	114*	93.67	2	–	–	7
1969	England	23	35	4	989	88*	31.90	–	6	2	8
1970	England	19	31	3	1242	111	44.36	4	5	2	6
1971/72	Aust & NZ	13	20	3	870	163*	51.18	4	3	1	6
1971	England	21	38	5	1130	136	34.24	1	9	4	7
1972	England	15	26	4	784	107	35.64	2	4	–	5
1972/73	Rhodesia	2	4	1	129	116	43.00	1	–	–	2
1973	England	19	27	1	587	97	22.58	–	2	2	3
1974	England	18	26	3	1026	227	44.61	2	4	1	4
1975	England	20	34	6	1225	97*	43.75	–	11	1	7
1976	England	15	26	6	840	113	42.00	4	2	1	9
1977	England	22	36	7	1257	156*	43.34	1	9	4	11
1978	England	17	22	5	728	146*	42.82	1	2	1	4
1979	England	7	9	1	257	112	32.13	1	2	2	–
TOTALS		361	564	88	18882	227	39.67	43	98	33	211

2 Batting in Test Matches: Series by Series

1966	Eng –v– W I	4	6	00	256	88	42.67	–	3	–	2
1967	Eng –v– India	2	3	1	166	109	83.00	1	–	–	4
	Eng –v– Pak	3	4	1	150	81	50.00	–	2	–	
1967/68	Eng –v– WI	5	8	2	137	51	22.83	–	1	2	3
1968	Eng –v– Aust	2	4	1	263	158	87.67	1	1	–	1
1968/69	Eng –v– Pak	3	4	1	161	114*	53.67	1	–	–	4
1969	Eng –v– WI	3	5	0	162	57	32.40	–	1	1	1
	Eng –v– NZ	3	4	0	95	45	23.75	–	–	–	1
1970/71	Eng –v– Aust	6	10	0	369	117	36.90	1	2	1	4
	Eng –v– NZ	2	3	0	163	100	54.33	1	1	–	–
1971	Eng –v– Pak	3	4	0	241	74	60.25	–	3	–	2
	Eng –v– India	3	6	1	88	30	17.60	–	–	–	1
1972	Eng –v– Aust	5	9	1	233	50*	29.13	–	1	–	3
TOTALS		44	70	8	2484	158	40.06	5	15	4	29

3 First-Class Record in England – Batting

a For Worcestershire

	Mtchs	Inns	n.o.	Runs	h.s.	Av'ge	100s	50s	0s
–v– Derbyshire	12	17	2	650	113	43.33	2	3	1
–v– Essex	21	32	2	1197	163	39.90	4	2	–
–v– Glamorgan	23	35	6	800	156*	27.59	1	3	5
–v– Gloucs	19	30	4	996	101	37.15	1	7	5
–v– Hants	14	24	1	522	74	22.70	–	3	3
–v– Kent	11	19	1	446	107	24.78	1	1	–
–v– Lancs	14	22	2	708	146*	35.40	2	4	1
–v– Leics	11	16	4	452	103*	37.67	1	1	1
–v– Middlesex	17	26	7	826	104*	43.47	1	5	2
–v– Northants	13	23	5	559	84	31.06	–	3	–
–v– Notts	13	21	5	815	123	50.94	2	3	–
–v– Somerset	17	27	6	662	147*	31.52	2	3	1
–v– Surrey	14	23	5	1027	107	57.06	3	7	1
–v– Sussex	14	22	3	514	128	27.05	2	1	3
–v– Warwicks	24	37	5	1517	103	47.41	1	14	1
–v– Yorkshire	10	16	0	430	227	26.88	1	2	2
–v– Cambridge U	4	5	0	185	112	37.00	1	–	–
–v– Oxford U	7	8	2	458	102*	76.33	2	3	–
–v– Australia	2	3	1	39	22	19.50	–	–	–
–v– New Zealand	4	6	1	201	88*	40.20	–	1	–
–v– West Indies	3	4	0	158	72	39.50	–	2	–
–v– India	2	3	2	326	174*	–	2	–	–
–v– Pakistan	3	4	1	150	96	50.00	–	1	–
–v– Sri Lanka	1	2	0	148	112	74.00	1	–	–
–v– MCC	1	2	0	98	65	49.00	–	1	–
TOTALS	274	427	65	13854	227	38.27	30	70	26

b For England in Official Test Matches

–v– Australia	7	13	2	496	158	45.09	1	2	–
–v– New Zealand	3	4	0	95	45	23.75	–	–	–
–v– West Indies	7	11	0	418	88	38.00	–	4	1
–v– India	5	9	2	254	109	36.29	1	–	–
–v– Pakistan	6	8	1	391	81*	55.86	–	5	–
TOTALS	28	45	5	1654	158	41.35	2	11	1

c Other First Class Matches

	14	23	2	995	119	47.38	2	8	2

d Record in all First-Class Cricket in England

	316	495	72	16503	227	39.01	34	89	29

4 First-Class Record Overseas – Batting

a
In Australia	11	17	3	707	162*	50.50	3	2	1
In New Zealand	2	3	0	163	100	54.33	1	1	–
In West Indies	13	20	6	532	101	38.00	1	3	2
In Pakistan	10	12	4	524	115	65.50	3	1	1
In Ceylon	1	1	1	18	18*	–	–	–	–
In Rhodesia	8	16	2	435	116*	31.07	1	2	0
TOTALS	45	69	16	2379	162*	44.89	9	9	4

b For England in Official Test Matches

–v– Australia	6	10	0	369	117	36.90	1	2	1
–v– N Zealand	2	3	0	163	100	54.33	1	1	–
–v– West Indies	5	8	2	137	51	22.83	–	1	2
–v– Pakistan	3	4	1	161	114*	53.6	1	–	–
TOTALS	16	25	3	830	117	37.77	3	4	3

5 Runs on Certain Grounds in England

at Worcester	127	200	33	7479	174*	44.78	19	39	14
at Dudley	6	10	2	291	107	36.38	1	1	–
at Halesowen	11	1	0	15	15	–	–	–	–
at Kidderminster	7	12	2	242	104*	24.20	1	–	2
at Lord's	23	36	4	1150	81*	35.94	–	10	3

6 BL D'Oliveira – Test Batsman

1966 –v– West Indies

(1)	(2)	(3)	(4)	(5)	(6) In	(7) Out	(8)
1 Lord's	7	run out	27		203–5	251–6	D
2 Trent B.	7	b Hall	76	65–10 DL Underwood	221–5	325–10	L
	7	lbw b Lashley	54		142–5	240–9	
3 Leeds	6	c Hall b Griffith	88	96–7 K Higgs	49–4	179–7	L
	3	c Butcher b Sobers	7		28–1	70–2	
4 The Oval	4	b Hall	4		126–4	130–5	W

1967 –v– India

(1)	(2)	(3)	(4)	(5)	(6) In	(7) Out	(8)
5 Leeds	5	c sub b Chandrasekhar (Subramanya)	109	252–4 G Boycott	253–3	505–4	W
	4	not out	24		78–2	126–4*	
6 Lord's	5	c and b Chandra'kar	33	122–4 TW Graveney	185–3	307–4	W

1967 –v– Pakistan

(1)	(2)	(3)	(4)	(5)	(6) In	(7) Out	(8)
7 Lord's	5	C Intikhab b Mushtaq	59	60–8 K Higgs	283–3	369–10	D
	5	not out	81	104–5 DB Close	76–3	241–9*	
8 Trent B.	5	run out	7		75–2	92–4	W
9 The Oval	6	c Mushtaq b Asif	3		270–4	276–5	W

1967/68 –v– West Indies

(1)	(2)	(3)	(4)	(5)	(6) In	(7) Out	(8)
10 P of Spain	7	b Griffith	32		471–5	527–7	D
11 Kingston	7	st Murray b Holford	0		318–5	318–6	D
	7	not out	13		38–5	68–8*	
12 Bridgetown	7	b Hall	51	57–8 JA Snow	319–5	411–8	D
13 P of Spain	6	b Rodriguez	0		260–4	260–5	W
	5	not out	12		182–3	215–6*	
14 Georgetown	6	c Nurse b Holford	27		194–4	252–6	D
	6	c and b Gibbs	2		39–4	41–5	

1968 –v– Australia

(1)	(2)	(3)	(4)	(5)	(6) In	(7) Out	(8)
15 O. Trafford	7	b Connolly	9		97–5	120–6	L
	7	not out	87	80–6 RW Barber	105–5	253–10*	
16 The Oval	6	c Inverarity b Mallett	158	121–5 JH Edrich 62–6 APE Knott	238–4	489–9	W
	6	c Gleeson b Connolly	9		90–4	114–5	

1968/69 –v– Pakistan

(1)	(2)	(3)	(4)	(5)	(6) In	(7) Out	(8)
17 Lahore	6	c Ilyas b Intikhab	26		182–4	219–5	D
	6	c Mushtaq b Saeed	5		46–4	58–5	
18 Dacca	6	not out	114	66–9 DL Underwood	100–4	274–10*	D
19 Karachi	6	c Aftab b Mushtaq	16		309–4	374–6	D

1969 –v– West Indies

(1)	(2)	(3)	(4)	(5)	(6) In	(7) Out	(8)
20 O. Trafford	5	c Hendriks b Shepherd	57	58–4 TW Graveney	249–3	347–6	W
21 Lord's	4	c Shepherd b Sobers	0		37–2	37–3	D
	4	c Fredericks b Gibbs	18		94–2	137–3	
22 Leeds	5	c Sobers b Shepherd	48	76–4 JH Edrich	64–3	165–5	W
	5	c Sobers b Davis	39		42–3	102–5	

1969 –v– New Zealand

(1)	(2)	(3)	(4)	(5)	(6) In	(7) Out	(8)
23 Lord's	5	run out	37	50–6 R Illingworth	47–3	113–6	W
	5	c Wadsworth b Taylor	12		234–3	259–5	
24 Trent B.	5	c and b Hadlee	45	64–6 R Illingworth	301–3	408–6	D
25 The Oval	5	c Cunis b Howarth	1		118–3	131–4	W

1970/71 –v– Australia

(1)	(2)	(3)	(4)	(5)	(6) In	(7) Out	(8)
26 Brisbane	7	c Sheahan b McKenzie	57	78–8 JA Snow	336–5	449–8	D
27 Perth	7	c Stackpole b Thompson	8		310–5	327–6	D
	6	b Gleeson	31	51–5 JH Edrich	101–4	152–5	
28 Sydney	5	c Connolly b Mallett	0		201–3	208–5	W
	5	c I Chappell b G Chappell	56	133–4 G Boycott	48–3	181–4	
29 Melbourne	5	c Marsh b Thomson	117	140–4 B Luckhurst 78–5 R Illingworth	88–3	354–7	D
30 Adelaide	5	c Marsh b G Chappell	47	96–5 JH Hampshire	289–3	385–5	D
	4	c Walters b Thomson	5		128–2	143–3	
31 Sydney	5	b Dell	1		68–3	69–4	W
	5	c I Chappell b Lillee	47	69–5 R Illingworth	158–3	251–6	

1970/71 −v− New Zealand

(1)	(2)	(3)	(4)	(5)	(6) In	(7) Out	(8)
32 Christchurch				64−4			
				JH Hampshire			
	5	b Shrimpton	100	93−5 R Illingworth	31−3	213−6	W
33 Auckland	5	c Morgan					
		b Congdon	58	52−4 MC Cowdrey	59−3	145−6	D
	9	b Collinge	5		177−7	199−8	

1971 −v− Pakistan

(1)	(2)	(3)	(4)	(5)	(6)	(7)	(8)
34 Edgbaston	5	c Mushtaq					
		b Intikhab	73	66−4 BW			
				Luckhurst	46−3	148−6	D
	5	c Mushtaq b Asif	22		169−3	218−4	
35 Lord's	−	did not bat					D
36 Leeds	5	b Intikhab	74	135−4 G Boycott	74−3	209−4	W
	5	c Wasim b Salim	72	106−6			
				R Illingworth	112−3	248−6	

1971 −v− India

(1)	(2)	(3)	(4)	(5)	(6)	(7)	(8)
37 Lord's	5	c Solkar					
		b Chandra'r	4		56−3	61−4	D
	5	b Bedi	30		70−3	117−4	
38 O. Trafford	5	c Gavaskar					
		b Abid A.	12		25−3	41−4	D
	5	not out	23		212−3	245−3*	
39 The Oval	5	c Mankad					
		b Chandra'r	2		135−3	139−4	L
	5	c sub					
		b Venkat'avan	17		24−3	49−4	

1972 −v− Australia

(1)	(2)	(3)	(4)	(5)	(6)	(7)	(8)
40 O. Trafford	5	b G Chappell	23		99−3	127−5	W
	5	c Watson					
		b Lillee	37	59−4 MJK Smith	81−3	140−4	
41 Lord's	5	lbw b Massie	32		28−3	84−4	L
	5	c G Chappell					
		b Massie	3		18−3	25−4	
42 Trent B.	5	lbw b Lillee	29		74−3	133−5	D
	5	not out	50	89−5* AW Greig	200−3	290−4*	D
43 Lord's	5	b Mallett	12		66−3	76−4	W
44 The Oval	5	c G Chappell					
		b Mallett	4		133−3	142−4	L
	5	c I Chappell b Massie					
			43	80−4 B Wood	114−3	205−5	

Notes:

Test No.

1. Was run out when a straight drive from Parks struck his heel and rebounded on to the wicket. Hall then took the ball and pulled out a stump with D'Oliveira still out of his ground.

2. Last wicket stand of 65 in first innings was at the time the last wicket record for England –v– West Indies. First innings 76 contained 10 4s, second innings 54 contained 10 4s also.

3. First innings 88 contained 8 4s and 4 6s.

5. Maiden Test hundred came in 165 minutes and the whole innings took 185 minutes, and included 13 4s.

7. 59 included 1 6, 9 4s.

15. 87* included 1 6, 13 4s.

16. Reached 100* in 218 balls and 196 minutes. Total innings took 315 minutes and included 21 4s.

18. Scored 114 of the 174 added while he was at the wicket. Completed 100 in 256 minutes and full innings took 285 minutes, with 9 4s.

29. His 100 came in 303 minutes and his total innings took 345 minutes and included 11 4s.

32. Reached 100* in 211 minutes and was out 5 minutes later. The innings included 2 6s and 13 4s.

33. Suffering from a knee injury batted no. 9 in the second innings, JH Hampshire acting as runner.

In 70 innings D'Oliveira was not out on 8 occasions and his dismissals were as follows:
caught by a fieldsman 33: caught by wicket-keeper 5: caught by bowler 3: bowled 14: lbw 3: stumped 1: run out 3.

No bowler dismissed him more than four times in Tests and BS Chandrasekhar stands alone on this total. WW Hall, Intikhab Alam, AL Thomson, AA Mallett, GS Chappell, DK Lillee, RAL Massie all dismissed him three times. AL Thomson took only 12 Test wickets in all, at an average of 54.50 yet dismissed D'Oliveira 3 times in the 6 innings he bowled in against him.

Key

(1) Number of Test and venue
(2) Position in batting order
(3) How dismissed
(4) Score
(5) Partnership of 50 or more
(6) Score when innings started
(7) Score when innings finished
(8) Result of match, W=Won; D=Drawn; L=Lost

7 Hundreds in First-Class Cricket

1963/64 (1)
115   Commonwealth XI –v– Governor's XI, Lyallpur

1964 (2)
119   AER Gilligan's XI –v– Australians, Hastings

1965 (6)
106   Worcs –v– Essex, Worcester
163   Worcs –v– Essex, Brentwood
112   Worcs –v– Cambridge U, Cambridge
101   Worcs –v– Gloucs, Worcester
107   Worcs –v– Kent, Dudley
103* Worcs –v– Leics, Worcester

1965/66 (1)
101   Worcs –v– Jamaican XI, Montego Bay

1966 (2)
123   Worcs –v– Notts, Worcester
126   Worcs –v– Essex, Worcester

1967 (6)
174* Worcs –v– Indians, Worcester
102* Worcs –v– Oxford U, Oxford
109   England –v– India, Leeds
147   Worcs –v– Somerset, Glastonbury
156   Worcs –v– Essex, Worcester
106* Worcs –v– Sussex, Hove

1968 (2)
158   England –v– Australia, The Oval
128   Worcs –v– Sussex, Worcester

1968/69 (2)
102* MCC –v– Central Zone, Lyallpur
114* England –v– Pakistan, Dacca

1970 (4)
101   Worcs –v– Surrey, Worcester
111   Worcs –v– Derbyshire, Worcester
110   England XI –v– Rest of World, Edgbaston
105   Worcs –v– Surrey, The Oval

1970/71 (4)
103* MCC –v– South Australia, Adelaide
162* MCC –v– South Australia, Adelaide
117   England –v– Australia, Melbourne
100   England –v– New Zealand, Christchurch

1971 (1)
136   Worcs –v– Lancs, Worcester

1972 (2)
107   Worcs –v– Surrey, The Oval
104* Worcs –v– Middlesex, Kidderminster

1972/73 (1)
116* International Wanderers –v– Rhodesia, Bulawayo

1974 (2)
108   Worcs –v– Indians, Worcester
227   Worcs –v– Yorkshire, Hull

1976 (4)
103   Worcs –v– Warwicks, Worcester
108* Worcs –v– Somerset, Worcester
106* Worcs –v– Notts, Trent Bridge
113   Worcs –v– Derby, Worcester

1977 (1)
156* Worcs –v– Glamorgan, Worcester

1978 (1)
146* Worcs –v– Lancs, Worcester

1979 (1)
112   Worcs –v– Sri Lanka, Worcester

8 Century Partnerships in First-Class Cricket

(1)	(2)	(3)	(4)
1962/63			
144–5	45	with R Kanhai (110)	Commonwealth –v– Rhodesia, Salisbury
1963/64			
1227–7*	83*	with R Kanhai (72*)	Commonwealth –v– President's XI, Rawalpindi
1964			
103–4*	62*	with M Hill (63*)	MCC –v– Cambridge U, Lord's
103–6	119	with JS Pressdee (34)	Gilligans XI –v– Australia, Hastings
1964/65			
113–6	73	with DNF Slade (64*)	Worcs –v– Rhodesia, Bulawayo
1965			
191–4	101	with RGA Headley (113)	Worcs –v– Gloucs, Worcester
183–4	106	with TW Graveney (104)	Worcs –v– Essex, Worcester
153–5	103*	with TW Graveney (126)	Worcs –v– Leics, Worcester
149–4	112	with JA Ormrod (50*)	Worcs –v– Cambridge U, Cambridge
131–4	107	with TW Graveney (66)	Worcs –v– Kent, Dudley
117–5*	61*	with JA Ormrod (66*)	Worcs –v– Warwicks, Worcester
103–5*	78*	with JA Ormrod (39*)	Worcs –v– Middlesex, Worcester
112–4*	55*	with TW Graveney (59*)	Worcs –v– Gloucs, Cheltenham
1966			
271–4	126	with TW Graveney (166)	Worcs –v– Essex, Worcester
164–4	96	with TW Graveney (109)	Worcs –v– Surrey, The Oval
109–4	70	with TW Graveney (94)	Worcs –v– Warwicks, Edgbaston
107–8	123	with BM Brain (4)	Worcs –v– Notts, Worcester

(D'Oliveira scored 66 of the first 67 runs in the partnership (the other being an extra) before Brain scored his first run.

| 104–3 | 80 | with DM Green (81) | MCC –v– Yorkshire, Lord's |

(1)	(2)	(3)	(4)
1967			
252–4	109	with G Boycott (246*)	England –v– India, Leeds
157–4	96	with TW Graveney (99)	Worcs –v– Pakistan, Worcester
137–5	174*	with DW Richardson (44)	Worcs –v– India, Worcester
122–4	33	with TW Graveney (151)	England –v– India, Lord's
104–5	81*	with DB Close (36)	England –v– Pakistan, Lord's
1967/68			
154–3	66	with G Boycott (243)	MCC –v– Barbados, Bridgetown
1968			
121–5	158	with JH Edrich (164)	England –v– Australia, The Oval
114–4	45	with A Jones (99)	MCC –v– Yorkshire, Lord's
102–4	60*	with TW Graveney (81)	Worcs –v– Oxford U, Oxford
1969			
165–4	68	with JA Ormrod (125)	Worcs –v– Gloucs, Worcester
1970			
150–3	72*	with GM Turner (99)	Worcs –v– Lancs, Worcester
137–3	105	with JA Ormrod (45)	Worcs –v– Surrey, The Oval
132–4	111	with TW Graveney (62)	Worcs –v– Derbys, Worcester
131–3*	70*	with RGA Headley (55*)	Worcs –v– Gloucs, Dudley
130–4	101	with TJ Yardley (57)	Worcs –v– Surrey, Worcester
110–6	110	with AW Greig (55)	England XI –v– Rest of World, Edgbaston
104–3	51	with GM Turner (73)	Worcs –v– Lancs, Worcester
101–3	78	with BW Luckhurst (67)	England XI –v– Rest of World, Lord's
1970/71			
183–4	103*	with KWR Fletcher (80)	MCC –v– S Australia, Adelaide
116–9*	162*	with DL Underwood (13*)	MCC –v– S Australia, Adelaide
1971			
146–3*	79*	with GM Turner (90*)	Worcs –v– Warwicks, Worcester
140–3	40	with GM Turner (179)	Worcs –v– Pakistan, Worcester
135–4	74	with G Boycott (112)	England –v– Pakistan, Leeds
129–4	69	with EJO Hemsley (8)	Worcs –v– Kent, Worcester
121–5	97	with TJ Yardley (31)	Worcs –v– Warwicks, Worcester
109–3	56*	with RGA Headley (187)	Worcs –v– Northants, Worcester
106–6	72	with R Illingworth (45)	England –v– Pakistan, Leeds
1972			
109–5	52	with EJO Hemsley (61)	Worcs –v– Warwicks, Edgbaston
1974			
130–4	70	with RGA Headley (68)	Worcs –v– Northants, Northampton
(Worcs were all out 174. The first 3 wickets fell for 24, the last 6 for 20)			
125–8	227	with N Gifford (30)	Worcs –v– Yorkshire, Hull
104–5	89	with TJ Yardley (50 ret. hurt)	Worcs –v– Warwicks, Worcester
1975			
214–4	75	with JM Parker (133)	Worcs –v– Notts, Worcester
117–4	65	with JM Parker (65)	Worcs –v– MCC, Lord's
1976			
151–4	113	with Imran khan (76)	Worcs –v– Derbys, Worcester
143–4	108*	with Imran Khan (81)	Worcs –v– Somerset, Worcester
133–4	106*	with GM Turner (169)	Worcs –v– Notts, Trent Bridge
114–4	60	with PA Neale (143)	Worcs –v– West Indies, Worcester

(1)	(2)	(3)	(4)
1977			
165–4	72	with GM Turner (131)	Worcs –v– Somerset, Worcester
105–5	84	with SP Henderson (52)	Worcs –v– Northants, Worcester
104–4	74*	with EJO Hemsley (54)	Worcs –v– Somerset, Taunton
1978			
234–4*	146*	with EJO Hemsley (105*)	Worcs –v– Lancs, Worcester
1979			
119–5	112	with DJ Humphries (68)	Worcs –v– Sri Lanka, Worcester

In a total of 60 first-class partnerships of 100 runs or more, 11 were shared with TW Graveney, 6 with GM Turner, 5 with JA Ormrod, 4 each with RGA Headley and EJO Hemsley, and 3 with TJ Yardley.

Key: (1) Season
(2) D'Oliveira's score
(3) D'Oliveira's partner
(4) The match

9 Bowling in First-Class Cricket: Season by season

Season	Where played	Mtch	Overs	mdns	Runs	wts	Av'ge	5i	10m	Best Anal. inns	match
1961/62	Rhodesia	2	49	13	116	3	38.67	–	–	2/69	2/97
1962/63	Rhodesia	2	57	18	130	0	–	–	–	–	–
1963/64	Pakistan	5	136	35	395	13	30.38	–	–	3/42	5/94
1964	England	5	109.5	41	266	9	29.56	–	–	3/20	4/93
1964/65	Rhodesia	2	55	18	125	1	–	–	–	1/53	1/107
1965	England	31	469.4	167	979	38	25.76	1	–	5/41	5/41
1965/66	Jamaica	1	4	1	17	0	–	–	–	–	–
1966	England	28	763.5	264	1516	73	20.77	5	–	6/34	7/71
1966/67	Barbados	1	did not bowl								
1967	England	28	650.1	213	1368	44	31.09	–	–	4/39	6/71
1967/68	West Indies	11	226	59	542	11	49.27	–	–	2/14	3/23
1968	England	28	467.3	145	990	61	16.23	5	2	6/29	11/68
1968/69	Ceylon & Pakistan	6	62	16	133	5	26.60	–	–	3/9	3/31
1969	England	23	316.3	95	607	14	43.36	–	–	2/11	2/11
1970	England	19	351.2	120	766	20	38.30	–	–	4/43	7/106
1970/71	Aust & NZ	13	*192	34	569	12	47.42	–	–	2/15	2/36
1971	England	21	464.4	164	999	43	23.23	–	–	4/38	5/62
1972	England	15	270.5	69	607	24	25.29	2	–	5/24	6/42
1972/73	Rhodesia	2	51.5	8	175	3	58.33	–	–	3/58	3/86
1973	England	19	398.3	124	839	35	23.97	–	–	4/30	7/38
1974	England	18	345.3	105	697	40	17.43	1	–	5/49	8/64
1975	England	20	460	111	1278	30	42.60	–	–	4/38	4/76
1976	England	15	208.5	54	520	21	24.76	1	–	5/48	7/87
1977	England	22	272	78	617	21	29.38	1	–	5/50	6/137
1978	England	17	193.2	48	483	17	28.41	1	–	5/48	7/71
1979	England	7	122	37	275	10	27.50	–	–	2/15	3/72
TOTALS		361	6505.2 *192	2003 *34	15009	548	27.39	17	2	6/29	11/68

10 Bowling in Test Matches: Series by Series

Season	Where played	Mtch	Overs	mdns	Runs	wts	Av'ge	5i	10m	Best Anal. inns	match
1966	Eng –v– WI	4	160	48	329	8	41.13	–	–	2/51	4/128
1967	Eng –v– India	2	35	15	89	3	29.67	–	–	2/38	2/38
	Eng –v– Pak	3	50	22	85	1	–	–	–	1/27	1/27
1967/68	Eng –v– WI	5	118	34	293	3	97.67	–	–	2/51	2/51
1968	Eng –v– Aust	2	39	20	49	3	16.33	–	–	1/1	2/45
1968/69	Eng –v– Pak	3	25	5	55	1	–	–	–	1/28	1/28
1969	Eng –v– WI	3	75	26	169	4	42.25	–	–	2/45	2/91
	Eng –v– NZ	3	53	21	77	2	38.50	–	–	1/6	1/6
1970/71	Eng –v– Aust	6	*114	*28	290	6	48.33	–	–	2/15	2/36
	Eng –v– NZ	2	*3	*1	2	0	–	–	–	–	–
1971	Eng –v– Pak	3	99	47	162	8	20.25	–	–	3/46	5/62
	Eng –v– India	3	58	28	83	3	27.67	–	–	2/40	2/41
1972	Eng –v– Aust	5	83	23	176	5	35.20	–	–	1/13	2/36
TOTALS		44	795	289	1859	47	39.55	–	–	3/46	5/62
			*117	*29							
			5706 balls								

Best Bowling in innings: 36–18–46–3 –v– Pakistan, Leeds 1971. The only occasion of his taking 3 wickets in one Test innings. On a further ten occasions he took 2 wickets in a Test innings. Best Bowling in match: 51–25–62–5 –v– Pakistan, Leeds 1971

Of his 47 Test victims D'Oliveira dismissed SM Nurse and Intikhab Alam 3 times and 6 more batsmen twice. 29 of his victims were specialist batsmen, 13 middle order batsmen and only 5 tail-enders.

11 Analysis of First-Class Bowling Record

	Mtch	Overs	mdns	Runs	wts	Av'ge	5i	10m	Best Anal. inns	match
a In England										
for Worcs	274	4947.4	1498	10949	444	24.66	17	2	6/29	11/68
For England in Official Test matches										
	28	652	250	1219	37	32.95	–	–	3/46	5/62
Other first-class matches in England										
	14	246.5	87	639	19	33.63	–	–	4/43	7/106
TOTALS	316	5864.3	1835	12807	500	25.61	17	2	6/29	11/68
b Overseas										
In Australia	11	*189	*33	567	12	47.25	–	–	2/15	2/36
In New Zealand	2	*3	*1	2	0	–	–	–	–	–
In West Indies	13	230	60	559	11	50.82	–	–	2/14	3/23
In Pakistan	10	180	46	493	17	29.00	–	–	3/9	5/94
In Ceylon	1	18	5	35	1	–	–	–	1/28	1/35
In Rhodesia	8	212.5	57	546	7	78.00	–	–	2/69	2/97
TOTALS	45	640.5	168	2202	48	43.81	–	–	3/9	5/95
		*192	*34							
c for England in Offical Test Matches overseas										
–v– Australia	6	*114	*28	290	6	48.33	–	–	2/15	2/36
–v– New Zealand	2	*3	*1	2	0	–	–	–	–	–
–v– West Indies	5	118	34	293	3	97.67	–	–	2/51	2/51
–v– Pakistan	3	25	5	55	1	–	–	–	1/28	1/28
TOTALS	16	143	39	640	10	64.00	–	–	2/15	2/36
		*117	*29							
d for England in Official Test Matches in England										
–v– Australia	7	122	43	225	8	28.13	–	–	1/1	2/36
–v– New Zealand	3	53	21	77	2	38.50	–	–	1/6	1/6
–v– West Indies	7	235	74	498	12	41.50	–	–	2/45	4/128
–v– India	5	93	43	172	6	28.67	–	–	2/38	2/38
–v– Pakistan	6	149	69	247	9	27.44	–	–	3/46	5/62
TOTALS	28	652	250	1219	37	32.95	–	–	3/46	5/62

*Denotes 8-ball overs

12 Bowling in first-class cricket. Best performances

5 or more wickets in one innings

1965
22–8–41–5	Worcs –v– Sussex, Worcester

1966
26.3–11–34–6	Worcs –v– Gloucs, Worcester
26–9–40–6	Worcs –v– Sussex, Worcester
30–11–57–6	Worcs –v– Essex, Romford
11.4–6–14–5	Worcs –v– Middlesex, Lord's
31.2–12–49–5	Worcs –v– Leics, Leicester

1968
9.5–1–29–6	Worcs –v– Hants, Portsmouth
27–11–51–6	Worcs –v– Gloucs, Cheltenham
25.2–5–65–6	Worcs –v– Leics, Worcester
26–11–39–5	Worcs –v– Hants, Portsmouth
33.1–6–73–5	Worcs –v– Glamorgan, Worcester

1972
15.5–3–24–5	Worcs –v– Somerset, Worcester
31–7–84–5	Worcs –v– Hants, Portsmouth

1974
21–7–49–5	Worcs –v– Gloucs, Cheltenham

1976
18–4–48–5	Worcs –v– Glamorgan, Cardiff

1977
26–7–50–5	Worcs –v– Notts, Newark

1978
27–7–48–5	Worcs –v– Gloucs, Bristol

7 or more wickets in one match

1966
46–16–71–7	Worcs –v– Sussex, Worcester
46.3–16–74–7	Worcs –v– Gloucs, Worcester
46.4–17–92–7	Worcs –v– Leics, Leicester

1968
35.5–12–68–11	Worcs –v– Hants, Portsmouth
41.2–13–80–10	Worcs –v– Gloucs, Cheltenham

1970
43.4–12–106–7	England XI –v– Rest of World, Trent Bridge

1973
25–12–38–7	Worcs –v– Essex, Chelmsford

1974
33–13–64–8	Worcs –v– Gloucs, Cheltenham

1976
41–13–87–7	Worcs –v– Glamorgan, Cardiff

13 Other Bowling Performances

a In an Innings

8–8–0–0	Worcs –v– Notts, Trent Bridge 1965
21–15–11–1	Worcs –v– Northants, Worcester 1966
12.1–7–8–2	Worcs –v– Glamorgan, Worcester 1971
17–6–17–2	Worcs –v– Yorkshire, Worcester 1973
14–10–8–3	Worcs –v– Essex, Chelmsford 1973
10–4–8–2	Worcs –v– Yorkshire, Hull 1974
11–4–11–1	Worcs –v– Gloucs, Worcester 1979

b In a Test Match
In an Innings

36–18–46–3	–v– Pakistan, Leeds 1971

In a Match

51–25–62–5	–v– Pakistan, Leeds 1971
64–22–128–4	–v– West Indies, Trent Bridge 1966

14 Runs for Worcs in First-Class Matches

In England	274	427	65	13854	227	38.27	30	70	26
Overseas	3	6	0	229	101	38.17	1	1	–
	227	443	65	14083	227	38.27	31	71	26

D'Oliveira's total of runs places him 13th among Worcs batsmen, while his 31 centuries put him in sixth place.

15 Wickets for Worcs in First-Class Matches

In England	4947.4	1498	10949	444	24.66	17	2	6/29	11/68
Overseas	56	19	142	1	–	–	–	1/53	1/107
	5006.4	1517	11091	445	24.92	17	2	6/29	11/68

16 Catches for Worcs in First-Class Matches

In England	156
Overseas	3
	159

17 Performances in limited overs competitions for Worcs

a Gillette Cup: 1965–78

Mtch	Inn	n.o.	Runs	h.s.	Av'ge	100	50	ct.	Overs	mdns	Runs	wts	Av'ge	5in	b/b
27	26	2	610	102	25.42	1	3	6	280.3	48	783	37	21.16	–	4/18

50s in Gillette Cup
50 –v– Sussex, Hove 1972
54 –v– Warwicks, Edgebaston 1973
51 –v– Leics, Worcester 1973
102 –v– Sussex, Hove 1974

4 wkts in a match
12–2–18–4 –v– Notts, Worcester 1974
12–2–32–4 –v– Essex, Worcester 1975

Man of the Match Awards (6)
–v– Oxon, Cowley 1970 32*: 12–6–9–0–: Worcs won
–v– Sussex, Hove 1972: 50: 12–1–26–1: 1ct: Worcs won
–v– Surrey, Worcester 1972: 45*: 10–2–17–3: Worcs won
–v– Leics, Worcester 1973: 51: 9.5–0–30–2: 1ct: Worcs won
–v– Sussex, Hove 1974: 102: 6–2–11–1: Worcs won
–v– Notts, Worcester 1974: 8: 12–2–18–4: Worcs won

b Benson & Hedges Cup: 1972–79

Mtch	Inn	n.o.	Runs	h.s.	Av'ge	100	50	ct.	Overs	mdns	Runs	wts	Av'ge	5in	b/b
33	30	4	890	84	34.23	–	8	6	291.4	52	794	33	24.06	–	4/6

50s in Benson & Hedges
52 –v– Leics, Worcester 1972

84 –v– Middlesex, Lord's 1974

59* –v– Leics, Worcester 1974
69 –v– Warwicks, Worcester 1974
72* –v– Minor Cos West, Worcester 1976
63 –v– Leics, Worcester 1976
50 –v– Kent, Lord's 1976
58 –v– Glamorgan, Swansea 1977

4 wkts in a match
10–2–23–4 –v– Oxford & Cambridge, Cambridge 1975
9.5–4–6–4 –v– Minor Cos. South, H. Wycombe 1979

Man of Match Awards (2)
–v– Leics, Worcester 1974: 59*: 11–0–18–2: 1ct Worcs won
–v– Middlesex, Lord's 1974: 84: 11–1–61–2: Worcs won

c John Player League 1969–79

Mtch	Inn	n.o.	Runs	h.s.	Av'ge	100	50	ct	Overs	mdns	Runs	wts	Av'ge	5in	b/b
120	108	12	2137	100	22.26	1	7	31	690.3	–	2706	113	23.95	1	5/26

50 in John Player League
82 –v– Kent, Dudley 1969
52 –v– Northants, Dudley 1971
68* –v– Notts, Dudley 1973
100 –v– Surrey, Byfleet 1973
69* –v– Yorkshire, Huddersfield 1976
56 –v– Notts, Trent Bridge 1976
66 –v– Hants, Portsmouth 1976
57 –v– Kent, Worcester 1976

4 wkts in a match
7.3–1–37–4 –v– Derby, Worcester 1971
6–1–26–5–v–Gloucs, Lydney 1972
8–1–16–4 –v– Essex, Chelmsford 1973

Total of 49 sixes in John Player League is highest for Worcs in the competition.

18 BL D'Oliveira in South Africa – non-white cricket

BL D'Oliveira's first appearance in important non-white cricket in South Africa was for Western Province in the Sir David Harris Tournament in 1946/47. During his whole career in South Africa he is reputed to have scored 80 centuries and averaged over 60 throughout his career. There follows a short résumé of his performances in the best class of non-white cricket in South Africa.

a Test Matches

1956/57: South Africa –v– Kenya Asians: (Capt)
2   4   1   159   53.00   70   –   1   did not bowl
50s: 70 (in 66 mins) at Hartleyvale, Cape Town.

1958: S. Africa in East Africa & Rhodesia: (Capt)
3   5   0   288 57.60   139   1   2   2   61–21–109–7   15.57

100s: 139 (in 183 mins) –v– Kenya at Sikh Union Ground, Nairobi 1st Test
50s: 96 –v– Kenya at Sikh Union Ground, Nairobi 2nd Test
      50 –v– Kenya at Bhora Club, Mombasa 3rd Test

Record – all matches: 648 runs (46.28): h.s. 139: 25 wkts for 298 (11.92)

b South African Cricket Tournament (Inter-Racial)

Record for South African Coloureds –v– Malays, Indians, Bantus
1953: 178 runs, av. 44.50: h.s. 75: 2 wkts for 21 runs av. 10.50
1955: 182 runs, av. 91.00: h.s. 153: 0 wkts for 45 runs
1958: 212 runs, av. 53.00: h.s. 102: 4 wkts for 31 runs av. 7.75
Record: 572 runs, av. 57.20: h.s. 153: 6 wkts for 97 runs av. 16.17

NB: This was played for the Dadabhai Brothers Trophy from 1951 to 1958. It was then discontinued and in 1961 a Tournament was commenced for the same Trophy for competition between the Provinces.

c Important non First-Class tour

D'Oliveira's Team in South Africa, 1966/67
435 runs av. 62.14: h.s. 101: 7 wkts for 41 runs av. 5.86
100s: 101 (in 74 mins,16 4s, 2 6s) –v– Transvaal Federation, Natalspruit
50s: 82 (in 81 mins, 8 4s, 2 6s) –v– Abed's XI, Durban
      75 & 69 –v– Abed's XI, Green Point Track, Cape Town
      66 –v– W. Province Invitation, Green Point, Cape Town

d Other Tours – First-Class and non First-Class matches

Commonwealth in East Africa & Rhodesia, 1961/62
All matches: 357 runs av. 51.00: h.s. 101: 10 wkts for 157 runs av. 15.70
100: 100 (in 64 mins) –v– East Africa, Nairobi
(Hit 5 6s and completed his second fifty runs in 15 balls.)
50: 69 –v– HA Collins' XI, Nukuru, Kenya
Commonwealth in Greece, Rhodesia, East Africa & Malaya, 1962/63
All matches: 536 runs, av. 48.72: h.s. 119: 18 wkts for 301 runs av. 16.72
100: 119 –v– Salangor XI, Kuala Lumpur
50s: 75 –v– East Africa, Nairobi
      73 –v– Malaya, Singapore
      53 –v– Malaya, Kuala Lumpur

19 BL D'Oliveira in League Cricket in England

Central Lancashire League – Middleton CC

1960	27	23	4	930	93*	48.95	321.1	70	832	71	11.72
1961	31	25	7	1073	127	59.61	228.2	33	734	31	23.68
1962	30	22	4	674	102*	37.44	373.3	58	1105	72	15.35
1963	28	22	1	986	87	46.95	340.1	82	867	64	13.55
TOTALS	116	92	16	3663	127	48.20	1263.1	243	3538	238	14.87

Birmingham & District League – Kidderminster CC

1964	16	15	6	706	115	78.44	305.5	79	720	43	16.74

Index

D'Oliveira, Basil